CLICK HERE

INTERACTIVE DEVOTIONAL FOR TEENS

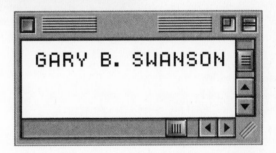

GARY B. SWANSON

REVIEW AND HERALD® PUBLISHING ASSOCIATION
HAGERSTOWN, MD 21740

CONTENTS

1

REDEMPTION

Day 1

"The Son of Man did not come to be served, but to serve, and to give his life as a ransom for many" (Matt. 20:28, NIV).

Organica

In the beginning the programmer sat down to a keyboard to write code for a new kind of computer. It would change things forever. It was a completely new kind of creativity. Balanced. Complete, yet becoming ever better. He wrote, and it was so.

He named the new program Organica because of its intradependence—that is, it depended on a system in which all the components were in complete harmony with one another. In fact, they needed that very harmony to survive.

And there was one more dependence: the programmer himself provided the power on which the entire system was based. Though all the components of Organica complemented, needed, and supported one another, the programmer was the one who provided the basic voltage. He was the one who plugged it in. It was something to stir the imagination!

All was well.

But the achievement of perfection carried with it an element of risk. Something could go wrong. Amazingly, there was no fire wall, no virus scan. If Organica's program had been written so that nothing could go wrong, it would have been less than perfect.

And because of this risk there arose in Organica itself a hacker with a virus in his mind. No one knows where this virus came from originally, but the hacker had the cleverness to write code that could invade and corrupt the whole program. He never realized that the power to do such a thing came not from his own abilities—that the programmer himself had created him.

The hacker wrote his destructive code and e-mailed it in a deceptively guileless message. It said merely this: "Check out this Web site. It is guaranteed to change your life! Click here: http://www.etc."

One fateful click is all it took. The virus was activated, in place, and on its way. One click, and it began to eat away at the code of the very program on which all Organica was based. The virus would affect every file of the program, and every file would unwittingly infect others, until the entire system would crash.

The hacker was e-lated. Over time he assumed the ostentatious title "Lord of the Files." Through his own wit, he thought at first, he had begun a process that would e-ventually bring all of Organica under his complete control. Even after he realized, to his horror, that his own destruction would inevitably result from his virus, he continued to pursue its end. Such was its seductive power.

All appeared to be lost.

But then something occurred that could have come only from the original programmer himself. Unexpected. Beyond imagination. It was something that would have to originate from outside the self-destructing program—from *Inorganica.*

The interesting thing is that most of Organica had heard of such a place as Inorganica, but they thought it was merely legend. They simply didn't believe it truly existed. In their own limited way they found it difficult to grasp the possibility of existence outside their own program.

It is at this place that the story becomes difficult to tell, first because of what the programmer had to give up, and second because it defies language itself. The programmer willingly jacked into the program he himself had created and entered the dying Organica.

In doing so, he didn't leave behind his inorganic qualities. He somehow became existent in both ways, yet in doing so, he gave up something of himself that he could never completely reclaim. It is what in Organica one would call a bittersweet arrangement.

The code had been written so that the only way to scan for and erase the virus was for one file to remain, in the end, virus-free. And that is what the programmer had done. Now he entered Organica, resisted the virus, and removed it e-ternally!

➤ How is "service" defined in this parable?

➤ How is the Internet like or unlike God's created universe?

➤ Find and highlight five biblical passages that describe Jesus' role as your Savior.

Day 2

"God . . . made himself nothing, taking the very nature of a servant, being made in human likeness. And being found in appearance as a man, he humbled himself and became obedient to death—even death on a cross!" (Phil. 2:6-8, NIV).

TIME GARMENT

There was no way it would fit—
        He knew that from the start.
But, all things being possible,
        He clothed His frame of infinity
                in a thirty-year garment.
It pinched and scratched
    and strained at every seam
    and stretched the fabric
            of human time so far
                that it will never be the same.

➤ How is the wearing of a garment similar to servanthood?

⚑ When was the last time you thought about how alien the world has become to Jesus?

⚑ For a week place the newest garment of your wardrobe where it will remind you of the sacrifice that Jesus made for you.

Day 3

"I know that nothing good lives in me, that is, in my sinful nature. For I have the desire to do what is good, but I cannot carry it out" (Rom. 7:18, NIV).

Born Losers

Ask Australian Bruce Bracknell if he's out of his tree, and he'd have to admit that he is—far more often than he'd like to be.

Bruce is a fruit picker who falls out of trees—a lot! So clumsy is he that he's broken his nose, his skull, and every one of his ribs, as well as every bone in both arms and legs (not all at once, of course).

To make matters worse, it can be pretty dangerous for others to be anywhere near Bruce while he's working. As a result of his many losing bouts with gravity, he's broken the bones of five other people, two dogs, a horse, and a koala. You'd think the insurance companies would pay him to stay out of trees.

Actually, in one important way we as human beings have a great deal in common with Broken-Bones Bracknell. We can't seem to keep from falling either. Try as we might to do the right thing, we keep returning to the acts and behaviors that we know are wrong—"as a dog returns to its vomit" is the way Solomon described it (Prov. 26:11, NIV). Not a pretty sight!

Yet this condition puts us in some interesting company. The apostle Paul, one of Christianity's giants, called himself "the worst" of sinners (1 Tim. 1:15, NIV) and said, "I have the desire to do what is good, but I cannot carry it out" (Rom. 7:18, NIV). Keep in mind here that Paul wrote these confessions in a world that also included

Nero and Caligula. Yet Paul *didn't* describe himself as "the worst of sinners *except* for possibly the emperors of Rome."

Actually, it seems that often those who are closest to God are the ones who feel the most unworthy. That's because they're comparing themselves to God rather than to fellow sinners. Job confessed, "I am vile" (Job 40:4); Abraham considered himself merely "dust and ashes" (Gen. 18:27). And according to the Bible, these were supposed to be some of the "good guys." We're not talking here about the likes of Judas or Jezebel.

The problem is that it's a little too easy to begin classifying people into good guys and bad guys, as though we're watching an old-time Western and judging people by the hues of their hats. In fact, the human condition here on earth is downright unanimous—we're *all* just a bunch of born losers.

A man walked into a pawnshop in West Plains, Missouri, to sell a bracelet he had stolen. The shop owner recognized it as one his own wife had recently lost in a burglary. He notified the police, who apprehended the thief.

In Charleston, West Virginia, a mugger, brandishing a knife, demanded money from a victim. Because the victim had only $12.50 in cash, the mugger accepted a $300 check. When he tried to cash the check at the bank the next day, he was arrested.

After stealing $4,000 from the Equitable Cooperative Bank in Lynn, Massachusetts, a man was captured minutes later in a hailed taxicab. He was easy to identify, because he was still wearing the mask he'd used during the holdup.

Hearing stories such as these gives us a smug kind of satisfaction. *What do you know?* we think. *Somebody finally got what they deserve. Poetic justice!*

But from a Christian perspective the issue of getting what you deserve can be a bit unsettling. The fact is that if we got what's coming to us, we would all be lost. "All have sinned and fall short of the glory of God" (Rom. 3:23, NIV).

If that's true, and "the wages of sin is death" (Rom. 6:23, NIV), then where does that leave you and me? Certainly not demanding that people should get their just desserts! No, the Christian realizes that there aren't "good guys" and "bad guys" on this earth; instead, we're the saved and the unsaved.

God's forgiveness and grace have mystified and inspired humankind throughout history. From a human standpoint, with our consistent emphasis on justice, divine grace simply doesn't make sense. Why in the world should we be willing to forgive others who have wronged us—even *before* they feel a need for forgiveness?

Your parents tell you, "Apologize to your brother, so he can forgive you." No one would suggest that your brother forgive you whether or not you're sorry for what you've done. Yet astonishingly, that's exactly what Christ did for us. While Jesus' hands were being nailed to the cross, He breathed the unfathomable prayer to His Father: "Forgive them; for they know not what they do" (Luke 23:34).

We are all, like Break-Neck Bracknell, out of our trees spiritually. It's the nature of sinful humanity. We are all fallen, all broken. Yet Jesus heals us, restores us, and has asked His Father to forgive us— even before we've ever felt the need to ask His forgiveness.

Thanks to Jesus, we will never have to get what's coming to us. Though we're all born losers, we can become *born-again* winners.

➤ How is being sinful like being "out of your tree"?

➤ What specific thing in your life should you change to help you avoid falling into sin?

➤ In prayer, ask God to help you make this change.

Day 4

"Our old sinful selves were crucified with Christ so that sin might lose its power in our lives. We are no longer slaves to sin" (Rom. 6:6, NLT).

THE CENTURION

"It seems so soon," Pilate said.

"Can the Galilean truly be dead so soon?"

"He's dead," the centurion assured the governor.

Pilate turned to Joseph

and with a curt nod

gave him permission

to remove the body.

"That's the finish of it, then,"

Pilate said wearily.

"With your permission,"

the centurion asked,

"may I speak freely?"

Pilate sighed but did not stop him.

The officer was relieved

but would have spoken anyway.

He had already

crossed his Rubicon that afternoon.

"I've watched a thousand men die like this—

but never has it gone as it has today . . ."

He fought back tears

he'd learned long before never to shed.

Pilate waited icily.

"One of the men came to notify me

that the time was near—

that the Man would surely die soon.

I too was surprised—

it usually takes so much longer

for death to come.

I've seen men linger

as if they would cheat death

by stubbornly outlasting it.

As surely as the soldiers

cast lots for His clothing,

He took a fearful gamble.

It's a contest with death

that all have lost—till now.

He rolled the dice,

and now we *all* have won."

➤ How does Romans 6:6 relate to the idea that "we all have won"?

➤ In what respects did Jesus take a "fearful gamble"?

➤ Think about whether you are comfortable with the idea that Jesus took a gamble.

DAY 5

"Jesus Christ . . . gave himself for us to redeem us from all wickedness and to purify for himself a people that are his very own, eager to do what is good" (Titus 2:13, 14, NIV).

IN BIG TROUBLE

At one time the police department in the city of Philadelphia came to the realization that for two years it had had no enforcement program for unpaid traffic fines. Authorities were shocked to discover that 75 percent of those who'd received traffic citations had ignored them. And they were getting away with it!

So the Philadelphia Police Department began to go after some of the deadbeats on the loose. The front office sent out a list of names to be arrested. At the top of the list was a fellow named Richard Canning.

Amazingly, Canning had racked up 301 moving violations in a mere two years. Among them were seven citations for careless driving, 15 for disregarding traffic lights and stop signs, 52 for driving an uninspected vehicle, 58 for driving without registration and title, and 85 for driving without a license. There was also an assortment of "lesser" violations—littering on the highway, driving without headlights, driving with a defective muffler, etc. Actually, Richard had more than 100 additional citations from more than two years before, but the statute of limitations had expired for them.

In short, it seems that Richard Canning had done just about everything you can do illegally with an automobile—several times over. He faced an 85-year suspension of his license and $59,585 in fines.

Canning must have felt a lot like the woman the Pharisees had caught in the act of adultery and had brought before Jesus to try to trip Him up with a question. They thought they had Him cornered with this one. Here was a woman who was plainly without excuse. She, too, was in trouble big-time. The law was very explicit as to how to prosecute such a case.

Based on one of the original Ten Commandments and sustained with the God-given Levitical laws, the issue didn't really seem to leave much of a choice. The verdict was clear: a person caught in adultery was to be taken outside the city and stoned to death. Capital punishment. And there wasn't any system of appeal in those days.

Yet, as so often before, Jesus did a startling thing. He stooped down and began to write something in the soil with His finger. When the crowd moved in closer and pressed Him further, He answered, "If any one of you is without sin, let him be the first to throw a stone at her." Then, returning to His writing on the ground, He began to recount the hidden sins of those very people who had brought the woman before Him. One by one her accusers made themselves scarce, leaving only Jesus and the woman alone at the roadside.

Jesus straightened up and asked her, "Where are your accusers? Didn't even one of them condemn you?"

The woman looked around. She surely must have been dumbfounded to see that everyone had disappeared. "No man, Lord," she said.

"Neither do I condemn you," Jesus said. "Go and sin no more."

One of the chief reasons that the story of the adulterous woman is so ironic is that we don't experience such forgiveness every day. Human beings go through life holding grudges and getting even. It seems that if we focus on the shortcomings of others, we won't have to come to grips with our own.

Yet in doing so we forget how much we ourselves have been forgiven. We overlook the implications of the words in the Lord's Prayer: "Forgive us our debts, *as* we forgive our debtors" (Matt. 6:12). We can be forgiven of our sins *only* as we are willing to forgive those of others.

Someone has said that getting even throws everything out of balance. That's because getting even leaves God out of the equation, and only He is able to set things right. In fact, He has already done so by allowing His Son to die in our place.

The story of the adulterous woman is astonishing and heartening for all of us. We may not owe $59,585 in fines to the city of Philadelphia. But we are all—each of us—just as guilty of sin. "All have sinned and fall short of the glory of God" (Rom. 3:23, NKJV).

That would be terrible news if we didn't also know that Jesus doesn't condemn us. Because of Him we can "go and sin no more."

➤ Why are human beings naturally not "eager to do what is good"?

➤ What recent news event illustrates for you most dramatically that human beings are not "eager to do what is good"?

➤ Think about a time someone forgave you for something. Write a short poem about the feelings that this forgiveness brought to you.

DAY 6

"As Jonah was three days and three nights in the belly of a huge fish, so the Son of Man will be three days and three nights in the heart of the earth" (Matt. 12:40, NIV).

INTERRUPTION IN THE PROGRAM

From the very start—
   the first downstroke
      of the lead baton—
  the melody took up its course,
     simple-sweet and deep,
       a single rhythm.
And then began—cacophanous—
   a dreadful syncopate—
     revulsive thrill—
  a wrenching out of tune
    in bold, discordant strains,
  until the lead could listen to it no longer,
    stepped down,
      and left the podium.

A moment at the very middle
  of the symphony
  when all fell silent—

cold and black—

each bated instrument poised,

unsure of where the lead

would go from there.

Was the symphony over?

But then the simple-sweetness surged

into another yet the same

and sounded chords that would end

the long discordance of it all.

➤ How does the subject of Matthew 12:40 relate to that of "Interruption in the Program"?

➤ What hope does Jesus' resurrection offer to those who have lost loved ones to death?

➤ "Interruption in the Program" likens Jesus' death to a silence in the middle of a symphony. Think of another appropriate modern-day image for Jesus' death.

DAY 7:

"In him we have redemption through his blood, the forgiveness of sins, in accordance with the riches of God's grace" (Eph. 1:7, NIV).

MAKING IT PERSONAL

Try some of the following activities as you complete this week's consideration of the subject of redemption:

➤ Ask an elderly person to share with you an experience in which he or she received forgiveness for something he or she did. Have him or her describe the feelings experienced.

➤ Find a library book of art reproductions that depict Jesus on the cross. Think about the way in which the artists' choice of color and design communicates this event.

➤ Sing or perform the hymn "Redeemed!" (number 338 in *The Seventh-day Adventist Hymnal*).

➤ Design your own "citation," modeled after one of the many received by Richard Canning in "In Big Trouble." Identify the receiver of the citation as "The World," the accuser as "Satan," and any other details that you think such a citation would include. Last, write the word "forgiven" in large letters across it.

➤ Read the chapter "Calvary" in *The Desire of Ages*.

2

HUMILITY

DAY 1

"The Lord's curse is on the house of the wicked, but he blesses the home of the righteous. He mocks proud mockers but gives grace to the humble" (Prov. 3:33, 34, NIV).

TRUTH IN A NUTSHELL

George Washington Carver liked to tell the following story from his youth about a deal he made with God.

"God," he said, "tell me the mystery of the universe."

But, according to Carver, God apparently had a plan for his life that was a bit more limited. "That knowledge is reserved for Me alone," God replied.

So Carver said, "God, tell me the mystery of the peanut."

"Well, George," God said, "that is more nearly your size."

God granted George Washington Carver his second wish, and he went on to serve humanity by developing hundreds of useful products from the lowly peanut.

By telling this imaginary story about himself, Carver demonstrates how God "gives grace to the humble." His original request of God was to understand the great mysteries of life. God told him that in order to gain any such understanding we have to begin with small things—those mysteries that involve issues that are more nearly our size.

George Washington Carver made the study of the peanut his life-work. And in this humble pursuit he earned the admiration and respect of the greatest thought leaders of his time. He truly achieved greatness by humbling himself.

↘ Why is it so often difficult for people to be humble?

↘ Among your own acquaintances, who would you say most emulates the humility of George Washington Carver?

↘ Copy the following quotation on an index card and display it in a place where it can remind you of your need to be humble: "Humility, like darkness, reveals the heavenly lights" (Henry David Thoreau).

Day 2

"It was by faith that Noah built an ark to save his family from the flood. He obeyed God, who warned him about something that had never happened before. By his faith he condemned the rest of the world and was made right in God's sight" (Heb. 11:7, NLT).

The Difference

Wonders of the world, they'd be—

if we could only find them—

Noah's ark and Nimrod's tower.

Monuments to man's achievement

(one that was, and one that wasn't).

Noah spent 120 years

in the rickety scaffolding.

He and seven others

had witnessed the dripping wreckage

of a world gone rebellious.

So he calmly sat on his hands

when Nimrod spread the blueprint

out before him.

Some thought Noah

didn't want to get involved,

because the tower wasn't his idea.

But they had too soon forgotten

that the ark wasn't his idea, either—

he hadn't saved himself.

➤ How do faith and humility relate to each other in a Christian's relationship with God?

➤ What is the difference between humility and timidity?

➤ Underline, highlight, or otherwise mark the scriptural references that appear at the beginning of each day's part of this week's readings. In your future Bible reading, watch for other examples of God's acceptance.

DAY 3

"Jesus grew in wisdom and stature, and in favor with God and men" (Luke 2:52, NIV).

WHO'S NUMBER ONE?

Kelly plays starting forward for his high school basketball team. Since he was in the seventh grade his coaches have drummed "We're number one!" into Kelly and his teammates so much that he sometimes wakens in the morning repeating the phrase. His friends greet him in the school hallways with an upraised index finger, and then they exchange a high five. "Beat Greenville!" "Beat Madison!" "Beat Springbrook!" they call to each other throughout the basketball season.

Kelly likes being on the basketball team. It sets him apart—makes him feel special. Kids at school whose names he doesn't even know slap him on the back. "Great game last night! We're number one!"

But lately something Pastor Richards said in a sermon has been puzzling Kelly. "We should put Christ first in our life," Pastor Richards said. He went on to explain that if Christ isn't first in a Christian's life, then that person isn't a Christian at all.

Kelly has considered himself a Christian for as long as he can remember. He has always tried to do right. But what does it mean to put Christ first? What does it *really* mean? Does Kelly have to give up everything he enjoys? Does he have to stop and ask God what to do in everyday situations? Does he have to think about Christ every moment of every day? Is there room in a Christian's life for dating? for hobbies? for part-time jobs? for entertainment? for athletics?

One of the best ways to answer these questions is to examine the life of Christ Himself. It's sometimes tempting to conclude that Jesus must have been the ultimate example of burnout. We read of His 40 days of fasting in the wilderness. Of praying all night. Of being so exhausted from His preaching and healing that He nearly slept through a storm at sea.

These accounts are reflections of Jesus' ministry, which was the most important part of His life—but certainly not the only part. The four men who wrote the Gospels did not put pen to paper so their readers would have an account of every aspect of Jesus' life. It isn't too important, for example, to know what Jesus' favorite color was or which hand He ate with or whether He had any hobbies. The Gospel writers' aim was to describe Jesus' ministry, because that, more than any other aspect of His life, is what draws people to love Him.

The story of Jesus' life, however, does provide some important clues as to what He expects of us as Christians. Although He was certainly a dedicated, driven servant of God, there is plenty of evidence that He was a balanced, well-rounded human being.

The physician-writer Luke summed up Jesus' childhood development in this way: "Jesus grew in wisdom and stature, and in favor with God and men" (Luke 2:52, NIV). In this way Luke was saying that as a child Jesus grew mentally ("in wisdom"), physically (in "stature"), spiritually ("in favor with God"), and socially ("[in favor with] men"). Christians who put Christ first will do what they can to develop well-rounded lives, just as Christ Himself did.

➤ How does humility fit in the description of Jesus growing "in wisdom and stature, and in favor with God and men"?

➤ How can a person lose humility in each of the following kinds of growth: in wisdom, in stature, in favor with God, and in favor with humans?

➤ Make a list of specific ways in which you should become more humble.

Day 4

"The poor will see and be glad—you who seek God, may your hearts live!" (Ps. 69:32, NIV).

The Soldier

Dropping his plumed helmet to the floor,
the soldier sank into the chair by the fire
in shivering perspiration.
His wife took up the helmet,
vigorously brushing it off.
He had always kept it gleaming.
"Were you there when it happened?"
she asked.
His silence had frightened her
since they'd come to Jerusalem.
She wished for the thousandth time

they could go back to Rome.

Like a great snake,

Jerusalem seemed to be
swallowing him slowly.
He had come home nights
always wondering,
the old assurances
slowly slipping through his fingers,
always asking questions
he was incapable of.
    His eyes looked through the fire
to something far beyond,
as though he could see right through the wall.
    "Were you there?" she whispered.
    He swept in a long breath.
"The birds were rioting
the way they always do
just before sunup."
She sat down across from him
where she could see his face,
and he turned away a little.
"Then everything just stopped,
as if to listen to some secret
told behind one's hand."
    There he goes, she thought.
Where did he learn to talk like that?
    "And then . . ."
He paused, seeming not to believe
his own recollections.
"And then a light
filled the hollow before the place.
It was so white
I couldn't keep my eyes open to it.
And a sound—I don't know
if it was the voice of a leviathan

or just the grating of the stone
rolling back from the mouth,
but you could feel it
hollow in your chest."
    "What was it?" she pressed.
She did and did not want to know.
    "I couldn't really see;
the light was too intense.
And yet—" He looked up at her,
his eyes glistening.
"And yet, you know, the air was fresh—
cool and almost musical—
and then everything went purple."
    He fell silent for a time again,
chewing at his lip.
"I don't know what happened after that.
I must have passed out."
    He rasped a sorry laugh
that choked into half a sob.
His clinched, sweating fist unfolded,
and there was a glint of silver.
    "They gave me this
to keep my mouth shut
about the whole thing.
But what happened out there this morning
makes this silver feel like sand."

➤ What did the soldier experience that made him "see and be glad"?

➤ How can someone seek humility and success at the same time?

➤ Find at least one illustration from nature that makes you feel humility.

Day 5

"Everyone who exalts himself will be humbled, and he who humbles himself will be exalted" (Luke 18:14, NIV).

Hula-hooping to Heaven?

Roger Bourbon entered a marathon in London in 1982 and finished with an impressive two hours 47 minutes. Actually, according to the *Guinness Book of World Records,* Roger set a world record that day because he completed the entire marathon carrying a three-pound-two-ounce bottle on a waiter's serving tray.

Thanks to Guinness, in fact, countless other people have competed in some of the zaniest contests imaginable. England's William K. Johnson holds the record for spinning the most hula hoops on his body at one time—81. Ashrita Furman pogo-sticked his way up and down the foothills of Mount Fuji in Japan—a distance of 11½ miles. Johann Hurlinger's record for walking on his hands has stood since 1900. Walking 10 hours a day for 55 days, he made the trip entirely on his hands from Vienna, Austria, to Paris, France—a distance of 870 miles. And in 1984 Arthur Ring set a record for skipping a stone across water a total of 29 skips.

For some reason people are always trying to find ways to be important in the eyes of others. We all seem to be looking for something to brag about.

This was the Pharisee's problem in Jesus' parable of the Pharisee and the publican. With a sneer he thanked God that he was superior to everyone else—especially to the publican nearby who also was praying in the Temple. The Pharisee appeared to think that he was the world record holder for righteousness. But what he didn't know was that righteousness isn't a competitive sport. In fact, the only way to win is not to compete at all.

➤ If "he who humbles himself will be exalted," when and where will this happen?

➤ If you were to choose one thing in your life that you need to change to become more humble, what would it be?

➤ In prayer, ask God to help you identify aspects of your life in which you seek to be exalted.

DAY 6

"We do not have a high priest who is unable to sympathize with our weaknesses, but we have one who has been tempted in every way, just as we are—yet was without sin" (Heb. 4:15, NIV).

THE APPRENTICE

In His father's shop—
    where chairs and doors and benches
        took their form
            from splintered wood
            and blistered hands—
    His father smiled distractedly
    and said that aching hands
        are sometimes what you have to pay
          to be a carpenter.
How curiously the apprentice Son
    must have touched the nails
    and—grimly fascinated—
        watched His father drive
          them into the yielding wood.
Could He have known
    that with such nails—

and bleeding hands—

He would someday build

a door Himself

that all except for Him

could gain escape?

➷ What evidences from Scripture can you cite that indicate that Jesus was tempted not to be humble?

➷ What kinds of work today do you consider to be humble?

➷ Name a world leader or celebrity who you think exemplifies humility best.

Day 7

"The Lord takes delight in his people; he crowns the humble with salvation" (Ps. 149:4, NIV).

MAKING IT PERSONAL

Try one or more of the following activities as you complete this week's consideration of the subject of humility:

➷ Imagine that you have been chosen to list the contents of an archaeological time capsule that illustrates humility in your own time. What 10 items would you include?

➷ Using a Bible concordance, look up each verse in the books of Psalms and Proverbs that uses "humble" or "humility." Afterward write your own definition of these two words.

➷ From magazines and newspapers, clip artwork to create a collage that depicts humility.

CLICK HERE

- Explore the contents of your kitchen (pantry, refrigerator, etc.), and make a list of the flavors that you would characterize as "humble." Think about why you included each flavor on your list.

- Browse through the sports and entertainment sections of a daily newspaper. Think about the impact of the photos and articles in these sections on the everyday reader with regard to humility.

3

FAILURE

DAY 1

"With God all things are possible" (Matt. 19:26, NIV).

FACING THE TIGER

With the support of the World Wildlife Fund, the numbers of Sundarban tigers—once near extinction—in West Bengal have doubled. This success story, however, had its drawbacks for a while.

As the population of these fearsome tigers grew, reports of attacks on humans in the area became more common. Wildlife-management authorities had to come up with a creative way to protect both humans and tigers.

Noting that tigers attack people only from behind, honey collectors and mangrove-forest workers began to venture into the tiger preserves wearing rubber masks tied to the backs of their heads. In the three years after the beginning of this two-faced technique, not a single worker wearing a mask was attacked.

The Bible says that the devil is like another fearsome predatory cat—"a roaring lion looking for someone to devour" (1 Peter 5:8, NIV). When you consider the awesome power of the devil, it's almost enough to make you give up any hope of escaping his attack.

Marjorie has asked for God's help in her weight-loss program. About 25 pounds overweight, she knows she's going to have to make some sacrifices—give up some things—if she's going to succeed. But Marjorie has a particular problem with ice cream. Whether it's fudge ripple, strawberry swirl, or rocky road, she loves ice cream in massive quantities.

Tom's biggest temptation is pornography. Even though he's a

faithful churchgoer, he can't seem to pass up a copy of *Playboy* on the newsstand. Then, when he's finished with it, he tosses the magazine in the dumpster with a sickening feeling of self-disgust. *What's the use of trying to quit buying this stuff?* he thinks. *I'm so weak that I always cave in!*

Temptation has a way of doing that to you. It makes you feel hunted, defeated, helpless. As Oscar Wilde said, "I can resist everything except temptation!"

But the Bible urges, "Resist the devil, and he will flee from you" (James 4:7, NIV). There is hope after all, and you don't have to be two-faced about it like the honey collectors and mangrove-forest workers. One of the most encouraging promises in the Bible is that God "will not let you be tempted beyond what you can bear. But when you are tempted, he will also provide a way out so that you can stand up under it" (1 Cor. 10:13, NIV).

With a promise like that you may feel almost invincible—until the temptation returns. "Wait a minute," you say. "I thought God wouldn't allow me to be tempted!" Sorry, but the Bible doesn't promise that you won't be tempted; it does say God won't allow you to be tempted beyond what you can resist.

Sometimes when we attempt to overcome temptation, we do it only halfheartedly. As Robert Orben points out: "Most people want to be delivered from temptation but would like it to keep in touch." We cling to some values and behaviors that will actually prevent us from withstanding the temptation.

Overcoming temptation is no easy matter. If you're really serious about it, you'll make a commitment to resist temptation *completely.* "Do not give the devil a foothold" (Eph. 4:27, NIV). Marjorie's taste for ice cream and Tom's problem with pornography may seem overwhelming, but there is hope. Through God's leading, they can learn to resist temptation if they remember that "with God all things are possible" (Matt. 19:26, NIV).

➤ How is the "two-faced" technique of protection against tigers similar to resisting the devil spiritually?

➤ What are some practical ways to avoid temptation?

➤ Think of three biblical characters who failed to resist temptation. What can you learn from the experiences of each of them?

DAY 2

"He who trusts in himself is a fool, but he who walks in wisdom is kept safe" (Prov. 28:26, NIV).

THE ACCUSATION

"Thou art the man!"

The prophet's eyes flashed,
and he thrust
    a brazen finger
        into the face
            of the world's most powerful man.

Silence settled in the court;
the whispering ceased;
white eyes rolled, and faces paled.

The prophet's finger
    impaled them all
    in limbo, squirming
    (never liked him anyway)
until the king, in weeping,
    freed them all again.

⬤ This poem refers to the results of King David's involvement with Bathsheba. In what ways had he not walked "in wisdom"?

⬤ What can you learn from the king's response to help you cope with failure in your own life?

⬤ Talk to one of your grandparents or to another elderly person about what they have learned from failure in their life.

DAY 3

"Though they stumble, they will not fall, for the Lord holds them by the hand" (Ps. 37:24, NLT).

THE FEAR OF STRIKING OUT

Babe Ruth began his baseball career as a pitcher. But somewhere along the line a perceptive coach, or maybe it was the Babe himself, thought that he could be more help to his team by swinging a bat than by throwing a ball. Interestingly, some of Babe Ruth's contemporary ballplayers thought he was crazy to make such a change. Hall of Famer Tris Speaker said Ruth made a big mistake when he gave up pitching.

The history books are full of people, however, who proved the experts wrong. In fact, sometimes it's best not even to listen to the experts. Grover Cleveland, a two-term president of the United States, once remarked, "Sensible and responsible women do not want to vote." (Now you know one of the major reasons Cleveland's face isn't up there with the others on Mount Rushmore.)

Charles H. Duell, director of the U.S. Patent Office, said in 1899 that everything that could be invented had been invented. Just for fun, take a look around the house and make a mental list of the things that have been invented since Duell made his fateful pronouncement. And back in the days of silent movies, Harry M. Warner, of Warner Brothers fame, once asked, "Who wants to hear actors talk?"

Sometimes we don't have to be listening to the so-called experts to get discouraged about something we've always wanted to do. Sometimes we are our own worst critics. Fear of failure or ridicule is usually enough to discourage us from going after a goal that our "reasonable" instincts tell us is impossible.

This was at least part of Moses' problem when God first told him to lead the children of Israel out of Egypt. Moses knew his limitations only too well. He remembered his failure when he had killed the Egyptian long before. "Who am I?" he asked, "that I should go unto Pharaoh, and that I should bring forth the children of Israel out of Egypt?"

Then he asked God what he should say. He claimed that the Israelites would not believe he was truly sent from God. He reminded God that he was not an eloquent spokesperson. It was plain to Moses that he was not a reasonable choice for the task that God was giving him.

God's answer to Moses' sniveling was simply to remind him of where all human skills come from. Surely if God made Moses' tongue, He could provide a way for him to overcome his problems of self-expression.

Like Moses, we can overcome our failures and our limitations. Babe Ruth said, "Never let the fear of striking out get in your way."

The key to Babe Ruth's philosophy is that everyone experiences some failure. The best hitters in baseball get hits only three times out of 10 at bats. Although Babe Ruth is one of the greatest home-run hitters of all time, he is also one of the leaders in strikeouts.

Appearing in his first professional football game, Walter Payton carried the ball eight times for a total of zero yards. He went on, however, to be inducted into the NFL's Hall of Fame.

The next time you feel like giving up because you blew it, remember that you're in good company with other "failures"—people such as Babe Ruth and Walter Payton and even Moses.

➤ In the experience of Babe Ruth and Walter Payton, what would you say is the difference between "stumbling" and "falling"?

➤ In a spiritual context, what is the difference between stumbling and falling?

➤ Watch a toddler try to walk. What can you learn spiritually from observing this situation?

DAY 4

"Why am I discouraged? Why so sad? I will put my hope in God! I will praise him" (Ps. 42:5, NLT).

JAMES

"I wouldn't bring this up," James said
to the small band gathered together,
"except that I'm afraid sometimes
we may forget that He was human—
the Son of God, to be sure,
but just as surely Son of man.
    "He was my own brother,"
he reminded them.
"Some have said that I
of all the family
most resemble my brother.
We ate bread together every day,
worked and played
around our father's workbench.
I've seen Him sweat
and cry and laugh
and sleep, so tired

you couldn't rouse Him."

    James lost his voice

in the remembering,

and then he found himself.

"It wasn't easy

living with someone who's perfect—

absolutely faultless—

trying to measure up

to the giant dimensions of His life.

Mother tried always to be fair,

but have you never felt smaller,

weaker, more ineffectual

than someone else?"

    James shook his head in wonder,

tears rimming his eyes in silver.

"Listen to me!"

A wry smile cracked across his face.

"Listen to who

is deifying Him now!"

➤ Psalm 42:5 speaks of "hope" and "praise." How are these words implied in the poem "James"?

➤ This poem is a testimony. How is it similar to or different from your own personal testimony of Jesus?

➤ In a poem, write your own testimony of Jesus.

Day 5

"Consider your ways! You have sown much, and bring in little; you eat, but do not have enough; you drink, but you are not filled with drink; you clothe yourselves, but no one is warm; and he who earns wages, earns wages to put into a bag with holes" (Haggai 1:5, 6, NKJV).

Hold the Fort

As a soldier John Bell Hood, a general in the army of the Confederate States of America, simply did not accept defeat. And of the thousands who served in the terrible Civil War, he was certainly one who could have been expected to give up.

General Hood lost the use of his left arm in the battle at Gettysburg and lost his right leg at Chickamauga. Then, trying vainly to defend Atlanta, he lost thousands of men under his command.

At any of these tremendous setbacks General Hood could have reasonably given up, could have allowed someone else to assume his role as a leader in the Confederate Army. But General Hood was committed to the work that had been entrusted to him.

Even after such personal setbacks and failures, he remained in command of his troops in the siege of Allatoona, where his 46,000 Confederates had completely surrounded 5,000 Union soldiers. Known as "the hardest hitter in the Confederacy," he personally led the offensive on the Union garrison. Tied to his horse and with a saber in his remaining hand, General Hood tried unsuccessfully to capture the garrison. He had to face yet another defeat.

Ironically, one of the defending soldiers in the Allatoona garrison later penned the words to the rousing Christian hymn "Hold the Fort." Remembering the courage of his fellow defenders, he wrote, "In our Leader's name we'll triumph over every foe." "Ho, my comrades! see the signal waving in the sky! Reinforcements now appearing, victory is nigh."

Christians are indeed soldiers in a war that has been going on for thousands of years. Like General Hood, we experience pain and disappointment and failure in this great war. But we know that if we do not give up, if we continue to "hold the fort" against Satan's temptations, we will be able to sing, "Onward comes our great Commander—cheer, my comrades, cheer!"

- How could it be said that General Hood earned "wages to put into a bag with holes"?

- In what areas of life are you earning "wages to put into a bag with holes"?

- Get in touch in some way (letter, phone call, e-mail) with someone who has been experiencing failure lately. Encourage him or her with some promises from Scripture.

Day 6

"See, O Lord, that I am in distress; my soul is troubled; my heart is overturned within me, for I have been very rebellious" (Lam. 1:20, NKJV).

Mount Hor

Aaron turned his weary footsteps
    away from his brother's leading—
        not in rebellion this time.
The time of dust
    and din
        and desert
    for him was over.
The hot, dry wind
    puffed up in his face,

blowing his whitened hair
into a glowing circle
around his head.
He slowly straightened up
and looked one last time
at the past
that lay beyond
the southern horizon.
Again he saw his brother
squalling in the reed basket—
little wonder she'd found him;
he smiled at the memory of it.
And then he winced
as the image of the calf
loomed glowing in his brain;
but the guilt
had been gone long ago—
he'd been forgiven;
Moses was that way.
So, with a deep sigh,
Aaron sat down
and leaned against a large stone.
There was nothing more
to do or say—
except that he was ready.

➤ In what ways did Aaron rebel against Moses' leading?

➤ How is rebelliousness like failure?

⤳ Ask a friend to support you in prayer as you seek to overcome some past failure in your life.

DAY 7

"Let us fix our eyes on Jesus, the author and perfecter of our faith, who for the joy set before him endured the cross, scorning its shame, and sat down at the right hand of the throne of God" (Heb. 12:2, NIV).

MAKING IT PERSONAL

Try one or more of the following activities as you complete this week's consideration of the subject of failure:

⤳ Create several copies of a bookmark, using the quotation from Hebrews 12:2 above. Share these with friends.

⤳ Read the account of Peter's denial of Christ in the chapter "Before Annas and the Court of Caiaphas" in *The Desire of Ages*.

⤳ From clay, plaster, wood, or another medium, sculpt something that signifies the overcoming of failure.

⤳ On a CD or cassette, listen to the contemporary Christian song "We Fall Down," by Bob Carlisle. Think about the way this song depicts the overcoming of failure.

⤳ Read a biography of someone from history who overcame failure in his or her life. Think about ways in which you can implement the principles of this person's life in the way you conduct your own life.

4

SURRENDER

DAY 1

"The light has come into the world, and people loved darkness rather than light because their deeds were evil" (John 3:19, NRSV).

THE TOMB PEOPLE

In a faraway land at the top of a beautiful hill overlooking a grassy valley stood a proud little country church. Its red tile roof and sharp noble steeple and neat orderly churchyard and clean white walls could be seen for miles around. On a sunlit morning its bell could be heard clearly, even in the next county. Everyone agreed that this was a perfect place for a church. It was idyllic.

This little place of worship sat nestled inside a neat wall, each stone of which fit so snugly with every other that the wall appeared even from a short distance to be whole. And within this wall the churchyard was inhabited by the tomb people. They had been there (we won't say "lived" there) for as long as anyone could remember, and they formed a quiet, closely knit little community of their own.

Over a great period of time the tomb people had gradually come to consider themselves an elect group. Because of this they ever conducted themselves with grave deportment. They had arranged themselves in fine, even rows throughout the grassy churchyard. Some were a bit larger and more elaborate than others, but it was agreed among them that all had a right to be there, that there was nowhere else they would prefer to be. Solemnity was the order by which they governed themselves. That was ultimately what they were all seeking: *solemnity*.

Though it wasn't a requirement for membership among the tomb people, many of them wore the proud mark: "RIP." This they considered to be a sort of principle by which they all attempted to guide their behavior. "Rest in Peace." There you had the essence of it all in three letters. How complete! How utterly elegant! Simple yet profound.

Through the years a succession of sextons came and went whose duty it was to care for the churchyard. With the greatest of effort they mowed the lawn, pruned the bushes, trimmed the walks, and cleaned the headstones. Over time this fraternity of sextons had developed such a finely honed tradition of excellence that the churchyard became a showplace.

And, further, the tomb people enjoyed an ever-growing admiration from the world outside its hallowed walls. On holidays, especially, visitors and guests came to the churchyard to place flowers and other offerings and gifts here and there. While they strolled around the grounds reading the epitaphs, these visitors always sought to observe with utmost care the unwritten demand for solemnity. And the tomb people reveled in this reverence. They thought they had somehow earned it.

Then one day a new sexton came to care for the churchyard. He had some rather radical new ideas for change. As he considered "RIP," he considered that "peace" was surely a worthy objective, but that "rest" wasn't exactly the only way to achieve that peace. He actually suggested that the tomb people didn't have to remain bound forever to their beloved churchyard, that if they wished, they could leave the confines of the wall and move about the country again. He pointed them forward to the possibility of a whole new life.

The tomb people formed a committee, got their headstones together, and discussed the offer thoroughly, but they were too rooted to their plots. They decided at last that the sexton's idea was just too revolutionary, downright upsetting. They'd prefer to stay right where they were.

One or two did accept the sexton's suggestion, and they were never seen in the churchyard again. But the great majority of the tomb people were too wrapped up in the affairs of the churchyard to want to leave. And that, by their own choice, is where they will ever stay.

➤ What caused the tomb people to choose "the darkness rather than light"?

➤ In what ways do even people who call themselves Christians sometimes love "the darkness rather than light"?

➤ Read "Tomb People" to a friend or family member who is a member of your own church and discuss the ways in which your own congregation may love "the darkness rather than light."

DAY 2

"Everyone who can see will be looking for God, and those who can hear will listen to his voice" (Isa. 32:3, NLT).

WHITE-LIGHT FEVER

He thought he had it made—
    big-rig license
        in the glove box,
    pedal to the metal,
    the Damascus milk-route run
        (home in time for supper).
But he was blinded
    by the high beams
        of the oncoming traffic,
    lost control and swerved off the road.
Witnesses of the crash
    say it was a miracle
        that he survived.
He was three days in intensive care

before they called a specialist—

some new kind of operation

that isn't even in the journals yet.

And now they say

he's on the road again,

driving under another name

for the other company—

even though his license was revoked.

➤ How could it be said that the central character of "White-Light Fever" was "looking for God"?

➤ Why is realizing the truth sometimes like being "blinded by the high beams of the oncoming traffic"?

➤ Compare and contrast "White-Light Fever" with "The Tomb People." Make a list of the ways in which the central character of the poem and the tomb people responded differently to light.

DAY 3

"O Lord, you alone can heal me; you alone can save. My praises are for you alone!" (Jer. 17:14, NLT).

IN STABLE CONDITION

In 1793 a third-year university student at Cambridge, despairing over an unrequited love, ran away and joined the army. Walking into the recruiting office for the Light Dragoons, he signed up as "Silas Titus Comberbacke" and embarked on what he hoped would be the greatest adventure of his life.

But it wasn't.

Silas soon discovered to his dismay that he wasn't cut out for the cavalry. He couldn't groom his horse, couldn't keep his equipment in order, couldn't even ride. And a cavalryman who can't ride a horse has got to be a little out of place. His superior officers certainly thought so—he was assigned to clean the stable.

Young Silas was no longer despairing; now he was desperate. He sent an urgent message to his older brother James, who had to buy his release from the Light Dragoons. Then he resumed his studies at Cambridge under his real name: Samuel Taylor Coleridge.

Though the rest of Coleridge's life was hardly exemplary, it can at least be said that the literary world gained when James Coleridge was willing to give his irresponsible brother a second chance and rescued him from the results of his own bad decision-making.

James didn't succumb to the temptation simply to let his younger brother suffer the consequences of his behavior. He paid the price to deliver his brother from his suffering.

From the viewpoint of our older Brother, Jesus, we are all—like Silas Titus Comberbacke—"in stable condition." Yet He sees in us gifts and talents and potential that we often don't even know we have. He paid the price to give us a second chance. "In Him we have redemption through His blood" (Eph. 1:7, NKJV).

➤ At what point did Coleridge (aka Silas Titus Comberbacke) realize that he could not save himself from the results of his own poor decision-making?

➤ What parts of your life, if any, have you resisted the need to surrender to Jesus?

➤ Evaluate your calendar for the coming month. What events or situations are you facing that you need to surrender to Jesus?

DAY 4

"Oh, what a miserable person I am! Who will free me from this life that is dominated by sin?" (Rom. 7:24, NLT).

THE THIEF ON THE CROSS

Could He possibly mean
what He just said—
that I will be in paradise?
Did I hear Him right?
He surely cannot know
the life I've led,
the reasons for my being here.
   If only they would quiet down
and let me ask Him
what He meant by that.
My arms are going numb;
can my mind be far behind?
   It's so cold . . .
Why can't they just leave Him alone?
I know what I've done,
so here I am.
But what can He have done
to make them hate Him so?
Why can't they see it?
How much plainer can it be?
Or is it just the pain
that's causing me to see

what I most hope for?

If He has said I will be in Paradise,

then only He can make it so.

➤ Besides the fact that he was about to die, in what respects could the thief on the cross have said, "Oh, what a miserable person I am"?

➤ In what ways are people today asking the question "Who will free me from this life that is dominated by sin?"

➤ Using a concordance, find at least three other passages from Scripture in which someone responded to the question "Who will free me from this life that is dominated by sin?"

DAY 5

"I have sinned against the Lord" (2 Sam. 12:13, NIV).

KITCHEN DETAIL

Gail Ennis was awakened at 2:30 one humid morning in Florida to the squawking of her pet parrot in the dining room. "What's going on?" asked her husband, Howard, as Gail got out of bed to investigate.

She tiptoed into the dining room with her two small dogs following her. Nothing there. But the parrot was still going crazy. Then, outside the picture window, she spotted a large alligator in the yard. She turned back toward the bedroom and called to her husband. "Howard, there's a gator out there!"

No sooner had she said this than she heard the screen on the window pop out. She turned, and with horror saw a seven-foot alligator slither into the room. *He's after the dogs,* she realized. One of the dogs ran back toward the bedroom, but the other headed for the kitchen. Gail grabbed the dog quickly, but slipped and banged her knee so hard that she couldn't get up. The gator continued toward her.

Suddenly Howard burst into the kitchen and dragged Gail and the dog to the bedroom, where he had a loaded gun. When Howard crept back into the kitchen, the gator hissed aggressively and charged straight at him. Howard fired the gun and dropped the gator on the spot.

Allowing sin in your life is like having an alligator in your kitchen. When that happens you can forget about going about life in the normal, routine way. It pays to have sturdy screens against temptation, but when you realize that you have allowed sin to enter your life, it's time to take drastic action.

When the prophet Nathan pointed out that King David had an alligator in his kitchen, David did not lie, cover up, or make excuses. He simply admitted that he had sinned: "I have sinned against the Lord" (2 Sam. 12:13, NIV). This is the first step in getting rid of the alligator.

- At what point do you think Gail Ennis came to the realization that she was helpless to save herself?

- What alligators of sin have invaded the kitchen of your life?

- Find a picture of an alligator in a book, magazine, or newspaper. Photocopy it and place it where it will remind you of the danger of allowing sin to remain in your life.

Day 6

"Don't even take along a walking stick, . . . nor a traveler's bag, nor food, nor money. Not even an extra coat" (Luke 9:3, NLT).

FUNNY GAME

Two strikes and two outs,
bottom of the ninth.
The bat weighed heavy
on my shoulder—
I hadn't had a hit all day,
and all my strength was spent.
Finally I surrendered,
called in the pinch hitter myself,
and that made the difference.
Somehow it raised
my batting average,
and I made it
to the all-star game
without even swinging a bat.
Depends, I guess you could say,
on how you play the game—
give up, and you win.

➤ What connection is there between "don't even take along a walking stick" and "without even swinging a bat"?

➤ In practical terms, what does Luke 9:3 and "Funny Game" have to say about depending on God for everyday things?

➤ Write three more titles that you think would be appropriate for the poem "Funny Game."

DAY 7

"He saved us, not because of righteous things we had done, but because of his mercy" (Titus 3:5, NIV).

MAKING IT PERSONAL

Try some of the following activities as you complete this week's consideration of the subject of surrender:

➤ Read carefully responsive reading number 799 ("Do Not Worry") in *The Seventh-day Adventist Hymnal*. Think about what happens to worry when a Christian surrenders his or her life to God's leading.

➤ Research the importance of a foundation to a large building. Think about how foundational it is to surrender your life to God's leading.

➤ By e-mail or post, send notes of gratitude to three people who have served as foundations in your life in pointing you to God.

➤ If you have a family pet, think about how dependent it is on the care and feeding it receives from your family. In a sense, the animal has surrendered its life to the family. Consider how this is like—and unlike—your relationship with God.

➤ In prayer, ask God to help you have the courage to surrender your life completely to Him.

5

DAY 1

"From the time the world was created, people have seen the earth and sky and all that God made. They can clearly see his invisible qualities—his eternal power and divine nature. So they have no excuse whatsoever for not knowing God" (Rom. 1:20, NLT).

THE HONEYGUIDE

In northern Kenya a nomadic tribe of people, the Boranas, have learned to communicate in a crude way with a species of birds known as honeyguides. These birds draw the attention of humans by swooping close to them, then hopping restlessly from branch to branch nearby while making a persistent call.

When the humans approach, the birds disappear over the treetops but reappear after about 20 minutes to call again and wait for the people to proceed. The Boranas follow the birds, all the while whistling, banging sticks together, or talking loudly.

This pattern is repeated for an average of about three hours, until the birds and humans reach a beehive. Then the Boranas enjoy the honey—a staple in their diet—and the honeyguides feast on bee larva and wax from the honeycombs.

Although accounts of this relationship between humans and birds have been reported since the 1700s, biologists have only recently documented it. Researchers have found that if they leave the hive to which a bird has led them without breaking into it, the bird will guide them back again and again.

This, in a way, is what nature does for the observant Christian. The wonders of God's creation repeatedly return us to the real source of life, Jesus Christ. And out of that experience of coming to know Jesus, we are nourished and refreshed in a way that introduces us to the possibility of everlasting life.

➤ How is nature like a honeyguide?

➤ How can you become more attuned to nature as a guide to God's love, even if you live in an urban area? Be specific.

➤ List three ways that nature has revealed God's love for you in the past week.

DAY 2

"By him all things were created: things in heaven and on earth, visible and invisible, whether thrones or powers or rulers or authorities; all things were created by him and for him" (Col. 1:16, NIV).

CREATION

Howling stillness sifted
in the endless everywhere
and filled the bottomless gloom
to the brim.
With a simple word
He cast, engineered, designed,
with materials from nowhere—
light before the sun,
evening and morning before the stars.
With a simple word
He detailed the verities
that would be questioned soon enough

and set about to mold

with His own hands

(no simple word this time)

a creature with the mind

to pose such questions.

➤ How could God create "all things" "with materials from nowhere"? Think about whether you have ever created something from nothing. What does this suggest about God?

➤ How does nature affect your everyday life? Be specific.

➤ Plant some seeds in a small pot of soil. Place the pot where it will remind you each day of God's creative power and love for you.

DAY 3

"The heavens declare the glory of God; the skies proclaim the work of his hands" (Ps. 19:1, NIV).

LET'S GET SIRIUS

In August 1989 *Voyager 2* swooped low over the north pole of the planet Neptune, more than 2.8 billion miles away. Hurtling along at more than 61,000 miles per hour, this spacecraft passed within a mere 3,000 miles of Neptune's surface, by *Newsweek's* reckoning. That's about the same as sinking a 2,260-mile putt.

On its voyage the faithful unmanned spacecraft sent back spectacular color photographs of the scenery along the way— Jupiter and its moons, the rings of Saturn, Uranus, and Neptune. It also signaled 5 trillion bits of scientific information for scientists to catalog and analyze. By the time the last batch of data came in from Neptune, the radio signal was so weak—a 10 quadrillionth of a watt—that it took

38 giant radio antennae on four continents to catch it.

Weighing a little less than a ton, *Voyager 2* finally escaped the pull of Neptune's gravity and is now continuing its odyssey into infinity. By the year 2020 its generators will be unable to power communications back home. After that it will never be heard from again.

The mission of *Voyager 2* into outer space has been described by scientists and the media as humankind's most successful ever. Yet as exciting as this accomplishment is, it could never hope to compare to the awesome vastness of space and of God's creative power.

On board *Voyager 2* is a recording of greetings in 60 Earth languages and one whale dialect. Scientists hope that sooner or later someone or something out in the infinity of space will happen upon the spacecraft and will be able to understand one or more of the recorded messages.

That seems a little odd when you consider that God is out there and has been trying to communicate with us for millennia. And it doesn't take 38 giant radio antennae to hear the messages!

➤ In what ways does *Voyager 2* "declare the glory of God"?

➤ How has God been trying to communicate with us?

➤ Browse through an encyclopedia of space exploration. What specific facts express to you personally the wonder of God's creation?

DAY 4

"There is only one God, the Father, who created everything, and we exist for him. And there is only one Lord, Jesus Christ, through whom God made everything and through whom we have been given life" (1 Cor. 8:6, NLT).

ARROGANCE

The gardener proudly shows

    the rose that trails

        along the split-rail fence

and smiles as though

    he himself designed

        its lace-veined petals

and contrived its subtle fragrance—

        a cloud of agent pink—

            that wafts across the yard

                on summer mornings.

➤ What does the poem "Arrogance" suggest about human achievement?

➤ In the past month, what examples have you observed of humanity's forgetting where its power to create comes from?

➤ Take a walk through your neighborhood and make a list of the ways in which nature speaks to you directly of God's handiwork.

DAY 5

"God said unto them, Be fruitful, and multiply, and replenish the earth, and subdue it: and have dominion over the fish of the sea, and over the fowl of the air, and over every living thing that moveth upon the earth" (Gen. 1:28).

TRIMMING YOUR WASTE LINE

Next time you crumple up a sheet of paper and toss it into the trash can, think about this: one third of all trash thrown away by Americans in 1988 was paper—newspapers, books, magazines, cardboard boxes, etc. It added up to more than 50 million tons in only one year. That's a lot of trees!

A few years back some environmentalists were accusing Christianity of being responsible for the poor attitude Western civilization has had toward ecology. These environmentalists said that readers of the Bible seem to believe they were ordered by God to "subdue" and "have dominion" over His creation. Those expressions, they claimed, suggest that humanity can do whatever it wants with the natural resources that are available.

But, as is so often the case, the accusers were not seeing the balance that the Bible offers on important issues. They overlooked the word "replenish." And, unfortunately, too many Christians have themselves overlooked this word.

It has taken the situation on this earth to reach a crisis before we have seriously taken to heart God's instruction to replenish the resources that have been granted to us. And that can start with each of us paying closer attention to what we throw out in the trash.

➤ How would you define the words "subdue" and "replenish" as they relate to a Christian's care for the environment? How do the two words relate to each other?

➤ In your own personal experience, which of the two words—

"subdue" or "replenish"—best describes your relationship with the environment?

➤ At your next meal, eat or taste some things that represent sweetness, sourness, bitterness, and saltiness. Think about how the sense of taste has often been overlooked as a way to illustrate God's creative power.

DAY 6

"God understands the way to [wisdom] and he alone knows where it dwells, for he views the ends of the earth and sees everything under the heavens" (Job 28:23, 24, NIV).

ASYMMETRY

In the beginning
God brought them together—
he to be the subduer
and the replenisher,
she to be subdued and replenished.
But somehow half the balance
was overlooked for centuries,
and he took advantage
of a one-sided relationship—
all taking and no giving—
and she has been left
molested, scarred, used,
to wait until God Himself
can balance it all out again
and renew the perfect union

He intended in the first place.

➤ "Asymmetry" compares humankind's relationship with the environment to a personal relationship. How are the two the same, and how are they different?

➤ To what extent will God hold us responsible in our abuse of the environment?

➤ Watch a sunrise or a sunset. Think about the personal lessons you can apply to your life from this experience.

DAY 7

"By faith we understand that the universe was formed at God's command, so that what is seen was not made out of what was visible" (Heb. 11:3, NIV).

MAKING IT PERSONAL

Try some of the following activities as you complete this week's consideration of the subject of nature:

➤ Listen to Fernando Ortega's recording of "Angel Fire" from his CD *This Bright Hour*. Think about how the song explores God's creative power.

➤ Create your own Web site that celebrates the wonders of God's creation. Include in it scanned photographs, scriptural quotations, and any other items that you think express God's creative power. Ask your friends to share the URL of your Web site with all their friends.

➤ Memorize a passage of the Bible that best expresses the way in which nature demonstrates God's love to you personally.

CLICK HERE

➤ View a nature videotape produced by the National Geographic Society or a similar entity. Think about whether any reference to God is made in it. What are some observations that could have been made to show God's awesome creative power?

➤ Visit a park where a naturalist conducts nature walks. Participate in one of these walks and make mental notes about the things the naturalist points out that show God's creative power.

6

DAY 1

"How long will you waver between two opinions? If the Lord is God, follow him; but if Baal is God, follow him" (1 Kings 18:21, NIV).

FOUNDATIONS

Once there were three brothers who never seemed able to agree about anything. On any given subject, if there appeared to be two viewpoints, they were creative about finding a third alternative. They were Republican, Democrat, and Independent; Chrysler, Ford, and General Motors; chocolate, strawberry, and vanilla. Ask them, "What is the color of that car?" and you were likely to get mauve, plum, and "Looks more like puce to me."

Their mother used to listen to them and shake her head and marvel to herself: *How in the world can these three sons of ours—all born and brought up in the same home—have turned out to be so different from one another?* At times it was kind of fun. But usually it was positively exasperating!

One day, early in their adult lives, Mauve, Plum, and Puce set out to seek their fortunes. It was time, their father advised them, that they establish their own homes. In preparing to do so, they had explored just about every resource that they could find about how to go about establishing one's home. They had consulted experts, checked the Internet, researched the library, and even prayed about it.

To offer yet another alternative, their mother, in her quiet, humble way, suggested that they should give consideration to a timeless, traditional story about two men, one who built his house on a rock and another who built his house on the sand. The interpretation of this tale had always been rather clear, because the Teller of it had come right out Himself and made the explicit application to life. It appeared that there was really only one prudent choice, and the mother hoped against hope that in this case, at least, the three brothers would agree.

Alas, not so. As in everything else, Mauve, Plum, and Puce read the tale of the two houses from entirely different viewpoints. While the poor mother wrung her hands and considered that maybe referring to the two houses had been a mistake, her sons set off. With four points on the compass, this allowed for the brothers to go predictably in different directions, even with one direction left over.

Mauve, ever the sturdy, sensible one, embraced the Teller's own original interpretation of the story. After an exhaustive survey of all the land available to him, he began to lay the foundation for his home on the most solid bedrock he could find. "No question what the story means," he declared with an air of complete confidence.

Plum scoffed. "That's a story from so long ago that it no longer applies," he said. "Today we have such advancements in engineering and construction that we can build anywhere we please." So he employed a contractor to begin immediate construction on a fine new home right down on the beach.

Puce had always considered himself of a superior intellect to the other two. "The story of the two houses *does* still apply," he said, "but you have to read between the lines. We're supposed to use our heads. If you want to extract the ultimate truth from that story, you have to consider the time in which it was told, the audience at whom it was aimed, the *milieu.*" He liked the word *milieu* because it always confused his brothers. He thought that using so sophisticated a word showed his superiority to them.

The result of Puce's reading of the story of the two houses was that he decided to build his home on the water. *What better protection against rain and flood,* he reasoned, *than to build your home so that it will rise and lower with the water level? The folly of building on the sand is obvious to anyone. And to build on rock means the house will stand, but what about the cleanup if a flood does come along? Who needs that? No, to build on the water, a houseboat—that has to be the answer.*

No such thing had existed, of course, when the Storyteller had first narrated the tale of the two houses. But modern thinking had provided an innovative solution to this rains-and-floods thing. "We're supposed to keep up with the times," Puce argued. "What's the use of scholarship unless we're prepared to apply it to everyday life?"

So the brothers built their dream houses, each in the location that suited him best. The three houses aroused a great deal of admiration in the community, for each was unique. The real estate section of the local newspaper ran a very readable article, complete with many photographs featuring the human-interest angle of the construction of the three houses. It began, "Once there were three brothers who never seemed able to agree about anything . . ."

Suddenly contractors and agents all over the area sensed a real estate boomlet. Clients began to describe what they were looking for in terms of the styles of houses that the three brothers had built: "I've been looking for a 'mauvelike' house"; "Don't you think that a 'plum' would look good in that location?"; "My wife just loves a 'puce place.' Can you find one for us?"

There was such a new interest in real estate that no one noticed the first light gusts and the first few drops of what later came to be called "The Perfect Storm." At first it appeared that it was just going to be another bit of bad weather, the kind of thing that makes one joke, "Those weather people never know what they're talking about."

But this time the storm grew ever stronger, seeming to build up in its fury. In the words of the old, familiar song, "The rains came down and the floods came up." It was just that simple, just that fearful.

When the water level neared their homes, Mauve and Plum had to clear out and head for higher ground. Puce, however, smugly watched the gathering storm from his living-room window. "I guess," he said, "this will prove who is the wisest of us all!"

After an unexpectedly long season of furious, howling weather, the storm of the century subsided at last. Mauve returned to his home, found it still intact, and began the work of cleaning up. Plum's house simply no longer existed, so he decided after all to rebuild in a safer location. And when rescuers went to see how Puce had fared, they found nothing whatsoever. His house had lost its moorings completely and been swept away in the angry storm, never to be seen again.

As a newspaper article stated, "It appears that there are only two choices after all."

➤ Explain how 1 Kings 18:21 agrees that "there are only two choices after all."

➤ How are the choices of Plum and Puce basically the same with regard to stewardship?

➤ Draw an illustration of the parable "Foundations," showing how the three choices are basically only two.

Day 2

"Can the ax boast greater power than the person who uses it? Is the saw greater than the person who saws? Can a whip strike unless a hand is moving it? Can a cane walk by itself?" (Isa. 10:15, NLT).

Ownership

I forget sometimes—
in fact, too often—
that none of it
belongs to me,
that the BMW
glittering in the driveway
or the four-bedroom Colonial
with green shutters
(albeit half paid for)
will never really be mine.

But such an arrangement

makes things easier

when you stop

to think about it:

since none of it

was ever truly mine,

losing it won't hurt so bad.

🢔 How does Isaiah 10:15 relate to the ownership of material things?

🢔 In what everyday ways are you an ax? a saw? a whip? a cane?

🢔 Find one of the items in Isaiah 10:15 (ax, saw, whip, cane) and put it in a place where it will remind you of your role in God's hands.

DAY 3

"Don't you know that you yourselves are God's temple and that God's Spirit lives in you?" (1 Cor. 3:16, NIV).

ROSES ARE RED . . .

Every February zillions of people exchange sappy greeting cards. In variations of red and pink, these cards express love in a broad range of messages, from "Be mine" to "I'll be yours forever."

But we sometimes forget that the words "I love you" are usually easier to say than to show. What really counts is the everyday actions that show our love.

Let's say that I gave my significant other a new watch for Valentine's Day. A day or two later I ask to borrow the watch and carelessly lose it. How is my valentine going to feel? She may come to the conclusion that I don't care enough about her to protect something she treasures a great deal. In the same way, if my Valentine agrees to "be mine forever," I'd like her to take care of herself, because, in a sense, she belongs to me.

Living for others means taking the very best care of ourselves. We owe it to them as well as to ourselves. This would mean that, among other things, we take into our bodies only the best things and refuse to take in those things that are not the best. To offer my "undying" devotion to my valentine really isn't much of a gift if I'm living a self-destructive life. This is probably what prompted journalist Ed Howe to say, "No girl ever falls in love with a guy unless she has a better opinion of him than he deserves."

What would happen if you offered your valentine a choice between two cars? One is in tip-top, well-tuned condition, and one has a better-than-average chance of causing problems somewhere down the road. Which do you think your valentine would choose?

When we run down to the store to pick up something for our valentine, we're usually looking for the best possible gift we can get for the available money. Whether it's a Whitman Sampler, a dozen red roses, or a musical Hallmark card, we want the very best, because our valentine is special to us. Why should our lives be any different?

➤ How is the way you care for your physical body an expression of your true relationship with God?

➤ For what human reasons do most people care for their health?

➤ On a computer graphics program, create a Valentine card from God to you. Think about what kind of message best expresses His love for you.

Day 4

"Shall what is formed say to him who formed it, 'He did not make me'? Can the pot say of the potter, 'He knows nothing'?" (Isa. 29:16, NIV).

JOANNA

Cuza stormed into the courtyard,
grabbed his wife, Joanna, by the arm,
and dragged her to a place
beyond the trees outside the wall
where they could speak without a fear
of being overheard.

"What is this I hear," he said,
frightened desperation in his eyes,
"about you traipsing to the tomb
and finding no one there?"

"It's true," she said. "I went
there taking ointments with Mary Magdalene
and Mary, James's mother."

Cuza shook his head.
"Rumors sail like angry clouds
above Jerusalem's roof.
Some say there were two angels in the tomb;
some say two men; some only one.
How can you expect me to believe
that what you say is true
when you yourselves cannot agree?"

"I cannot tell you anything of that,"

Joanna cut her husband off.
"Ask anyone to witness what he saw
the day Siloam's tower fell,
and some details are sure to contradict
reports from someone else.
Yet one fact is woven like a thread
through the fabric of accounts:
the tower fell!
    "And just as surely, Cuza, this remains:
The One for whom we'd gone
was gone Himself—
that part, at least, is sure.
To that we all agree.
What does it matter
who or what we found instead?"
    "I told you, did I not,"
Cuza whisper-shrieked,
"that your persistence in this foolishness
would undermine our standing
in the eyes of Herod's court.
And now you want me to believe
that, after all, He's simply come to life!"
    She fixed on him a look
he knew too well.
Its eloquence surpassed all other argument
and finally flattened any further doubt
he may have had.
He'd known before he even found her
in the court.

"Well," he said at last,

"the course of my career

as manager of Herod's house

will never be the same."

Joanna smiled. "You'll get used to that,"

she said. "All you have to do

is let the risen One

become the manager of *yours.*"

➤ How has Cuza made the same mistake as a pot who says of its potter, "He did not make me"?

➤ In what way is true stewardship a kind of surrender?

➤ Make a list of the material blessings that God has made available to you. In prayer, thank God for these, and ask Him to help you remember from whom they have come.

Day 5

"You nullify the word of God for the sake of your tradition" (Matt. 15:6, NIV).

Crosses, Pretzels, and Croissants

Ever wonder why we cross our fingers for good luck, or why pretzels and croissants have their unique shapes?

You need wonder no longer. Here are the answers to these conundrums:

➤ Early Christians used to cross their fingers as a means of asking for God's blessing on something without causing the notice of the pagans around them.

69

- Medieval monks first designed pretzels as rewards for good kids who had learned their lessons. They gave them their shape to simulate a child folding his arms in prayer across his chest.

- Austrian bakers first began to sell the croissant in the 1680s to commemorate Vienna's successful defense against an Ottoman Turk invasion. Originally shaped like the crescent in the Turkish flag, the croissant has become one of the most popular of baked goods around the world.

Of course, none of these symbols has any such meaning for us today. Our culture is rich with practices and products for which we no longer have any recognition of their significances.

That can happen in religion, too. Why do we ask a blessing on our food at mealtime? Why do we memorize verses of Scripture? Why do we go to church? Why do we return a tithe?

Now and then we need to ask ourselves such questions, or we may be in danger of nullifying God's law with our traditions.

➤ How is returning a tithe without knowing exactly why we do so like nullifying the law with traditions?

➤ What other specific ways have Christians nullified the law with traditions?

➤ In a single sentence, tell why you return a tithe to God.

Day 6

"Do not store up for yourselves treasures on earth, where moth and rust destroy, and where thieves break in and steal. But store up for yourselves treasures in heaven, where moth and rust do not destroy, and where thieves do not break in and steal" (Matt. 6:19, 20, NIV).

Toys

When I was seven
we went to Signa Nordlund's house,
an old friend of my grandparents'
who came on the same boat from Sweden.
She opened up a drawer to me
with six years' worth
of cereal prizes in it—
whistles, puzzles, metal crickets;
balloons and tops and tricks
(the Nordlunds ate a lot of cereal).
She gave me all the prizes,
and I felt as if
I'd inherited a fortune;
it nearly filled my shoe box.
But today my toy fortune is gone—
balloons exploded, metal crickets
snapped like plastic.
And I sometimes wonder
if the toys I have
around the house today
will be of any more satisfaction

in another twenty years

than the whistles, tops, and puzzles.

➤ What kinds of "toys" do you have today that will not have value in the future?

➤ Specifically, what are "treasures in heaven"? How do we store them up?

➤ Copy Matthew 6:19, 20 on a dollar-shaped slip of paper and place it in your wallet where you will see it frequently.

Day 7

"The purses of heaven have no holes in them" (Luke 12:33, NLT).

Making It Personal

Try some of the following activities as you complete this week's consideration of the subject of stewardship:

➤ Watch a television commercial very carefully and analytically. Write down three ways that the commercial communicates a spirit of materialism.

➤ Read pages 88-91 in *Thoughts From the Mount of Blessing*.

➤ For a full 24-hour period, write down your various activities. Evaluate your stewardship of time.

➤ Using a concordance, look up as many scriptural references in the four Gospels as you can that use the word "treasure." Write a single-sentence definition of "treasure" as it is used in these passages.

➤ Rewrite the parable "Foundations" (see Day 1) in the form of a skit. If you can, enlist some friends to enact the skit for a Sabbath school or youth program.

7

DAY 1

"For the body is not one member, but many" (1 Cor. 12:14).

FEELING ANTSY?

The English language hasn't been very kind to ants. We have the expression "ants in your pants" to describe a slightly irritable, unsettled feeling. We describe a fidgety, impatient person as being "antsy."

Yet the close study of ants has led researchers to respect and even admire these industrious little insects. "Acting together," says Pulitzer Prize-winning author Edward O. Wilson, "ants are among the dominant forces of our terrestrial environment."

Representatives of the 8,800 known species can be found anywhere on earth, except for in the polar regions. With a population of 10 million billion, ants outnumber mammals, birds, reptiles, and amphibians combined.

Without knowing it, the human race depends on ants in many ways. With the help of termites, ants turn most of the world's topsoil. They spread plant seeds and scavenge and consume more than 90 percent of small-animal corpses.

But perhaps most impressive is the way in which ants assume roles in their communities. There are soldiers, builders, nurses, farmers, and hunters. And all contribute some specific talent to the welfare of the colony.

Desert ants of North Africa carry back to the colony 15 to 20 times their weight in food. These creatures have no time to waste, because it takes an average of only six days before they get lost or are picked off by larger insects.

Christians, too, are supposed to work for the good of those around them. The Christian church is described as a single body, each of its parts working for the good of the whole. In this context we can learn a great deal about the kingdom of heaven from the hardworking cooperation that goes on in an ant colony.

➤ How is a colony of ants like a physical human body? How is it different?

➤ Of the different roles that ants play in their community, which best describes your role today in the kingdom of heaven?

➤ Take some time to observe an ant colony at work. What other practical lessons can you learn from an ant's behavior?

DAY 2

"You are the light of the world—like a city on a mountain, glowing in the night for all to see" (Matt. 5:14, NLT).

UPKEEP

This white picket fence
faces Market Street
and separates the neighborhood kids
from Mrs. Jenkins' jonquils.
Twice a year she paints the slats
so faithfully that people come
from clear across town
to see what white should be.
And I sometimes wonder
what Bentonville will do

when Mrs. Jenkins dies.

How then will neighbors know

what white should be

if their own fences are unpainted?

➤ How is Mrs. Jenkins' fence like the "city on a mountain"?

➤ How are God's people responsible for showing the world "what white should be"? Be specific.

➤ Listen to three pieces of contemporary Christian music that explore the role of God's people—the kingdom of heaven on earth.

DAY 3

" 'The wolf and the lamb will feed together, and the lion will eat straw like the ox. . . . They will neither harm nor destroy on all my holy mountain,' says the Lord" (Isa. 65:25, NIV).

WOLF IN HEAVENLY CLOTHING

For millennia the wolf has been considered by humanity to be one of the bloodthirstiest representatives in the animal kingdom. So much so, in fact, that the prophet Isaiah chose the wolf and the lion to show the utter contrast in behavior that animals—including human beings—will undergo in heaven, God's "holy mountain."

In recent years researchers have reported some interesting details about the behavior and social structure of wolves. A new pack forms when a young wolf leaves its family and sets out to establish its own territory. One wolf traveled 550 miles before it settled down to establish territory of its own. Packs usually number from five to 10, and an individual wolf's place in the order of things determines when it can eat from a kill.

Some of the most fascinating lupine research has investigated how wolves communicate. For a long time we've known that they mark their territory by urinating on fence posts, trees, and stumps. But beyond marking territory, the particular scents in urine also communicate to other members of a pack where the marking wolf has been, what it has eaten, and when.

And wolves talk. Using sophisticated sound instruments, biologists have assigned whimpers to friendliness, chirps to flirtation, and prolonged squeaks to invitations to group howls.

Contrary to folklore, wolves don't howl more during full moons. On open terrain a howl travels as far as 10 miles and is considered to defend territory against intruders or unite a pack during a hunt.

But whatever behavior a wolf may demonstrate on earth, we know that it will be as gentle as a lamb in heaven. And the good news is that we will be too.

➤ In what way is a Christian a "wolf in heavenly clothing"?

➤ How can we as members of the kingdom of heaven behave today more like we will behave after sin has been destroyed?

➤ Think of three other object lessons from nature that could illustrate the characteristics of those in the kingdom of heaven.

Day 4

"To all who believed him and accepted him, he gave the right to become children of God" (John 1:12, NLT).

The Nobleman

"The story of what He did here in Cana

at the wedding feast—

wine from six water pots—

had been flying around.

Everyone you spoke to had an opinion.
But when my son took ill
and I heard that He was back in Cana,
I sought Him out.

    "He shook His head
and muttered that we don't believe
unless we see extraordinary things.
It's true, I must confess.
But this time I truly believed it
before I saw it with my own eyes.

    "'Go your way,' He said. 'Your son lives.'
And somehow I knew my son had been spared.
On my way home
my servants met me on the road.
'Your son lives,' they cried,
the very words that He had uttered.
When I asked the hour
they knew my son would recover,
they said the fever had left him
at the very hour the Man had assured me
of his healing.

    "Now my whole household—
family members to the last servant—
believe He is who He says He is.
And, do you know,
for the first time in my life
I can see we've *all* needed healing.
It isn't as if we'll never face

pain and suffering again.

Physical healing isn't everything!

But now my home is whole.

For the first time in our lives,

it is a place producing music

in which we're all in tune.

We're living today

in the kingdom of heaven!"

➤ How does becoming children of God create an atmosphere in which "we're all in tune"?

➤ How can you know today whether you're living in the kingdom of heaven? Be specific.

➤ Observe some children at play. Think about what you can learn about the kingdom of heaven from the behavior of children.

DAY 5

"In My Father's house are many mansions; if it were not so, I would have told you. I go to prepare a place for you" (John 14:2, NKJV).

FROM TENEMENTS TO MANSIONS

John Quincy Adams, the sixth president of the United States, lived a long and productive life. Even after suffering a stroke at the age of 79, he continued for a time in public life, but his health was clearly failing.

One day a friend asked him how he was feeling.

"I inhabit a weak, frail, decayed tenement; battered by the winds and broken in by the storms," Adams said. "And, from all I can learn, the landlord does not intend to repair."

Clearly President Adams recognized his reliance on God for his life and health. He knew that true health—wholeness of body and mind and spirit—is a gift of God. Indeed, the only life-giving ability we have as human beings is to take the very best possible care of our health and thus—by God's grace—extend our time here on earth and lead fulfilling lives.

God created us to be healthy and happy. He set forth some simple, basic principles by which we can achieve the optimum from our time here on earth. We are instructed to be stewards over the blessings God has given us. These blessings certainly would include health. He meant for us to reflect Him as much as is humanly possible through the positive use of the wonderful bodies He created for us.

And if we are faithful stewards of the "tenements" that we live in, we will reap two rewards. First, we will live more enriching lives here on earth. Second, we will someday enjoy everlasting health and happiness in the kingdom of heaven.

This is something that John Quincy Adams may have been overlooking. The Landlord does intend to repair the tenements of our lives. We have been promised that we will live in mansions.

➤ What kind of "tenement" are you living in today? Be specific.

➤ If God's plan for us is to be happy and healthy, why is there so much pain and suffering, even for Christians?

➤ Write a radio public service message that communicates the benefits to health and happiness of being a member of the kingdom of heaven.

Day 6

"We know that if the earthly tent we live in is destroyed, we have a building from God, an eternal house in heaven, not built by human hands" (2 Cor. 5:1, NIV).

TRACKS AND TURNSTILES

I remember
  my first trip
    to Disneyland.
I rode the mules
  and the rocket ships
  and the bumper cars
    that ran in tracks
    with railings on both sides
    so you couldn't go wrong.
And I wondered how heaven
  could ever be any better
    than freshly painted
    fully automated Disneyland.
But the place closed at 9:00 p.m.,
  and we were ushered out
    through the churning turnstiles.
And as the uniformed security guards
  watched us go,
I finally saw the difference.

➤ In comparing 2 Corinthians 5:1 with "Tracks and Turnstiles," what is the difference between Disneyland and heaven?

➤ What is the difference, if any, between having fun and experiencing happiness?

➤ Underline, highlight, circle, or star as many scriptural references as you can find that describe the kingdom of heaven.

DAY 7

"My kingdom is not of this world" (John 18:36).

MAKING IT PERSONAL

Try some of the following activities as you complete this week's consideration of the subject of the kingdom of heaven:

➤ Write a song, psalm, or poem that celebrates your citizenship in the kingdom of heaven—a kind of cosmic anthem.

➤ Examine closely some artistic representations of the kingdom of heaven. How would you characterize these illustrations? What feelings do they evoke in you?

➤ Phone a friend and spend some time with him or her sharing ideas about what heaven will be like. In prayer, ask God to help you both bring some of the spirit of the kingdom of heaven to your own families.

➤ Read some of the responsive readings on the subject of heaven after Jesus' second coming in *The Seventh-day Adventist Hymnal* (numbers 748, 749, 750, 783). Think about how you can enjoy some of the benefits of the kingdom of heaven even now.

➤ In a quiet place, take some time to meditate on the text for today. Ask God to help you become a better citizen of the kingdom of heaven today.

8

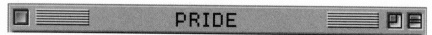

PRIDE

Day 1

"The fool says in his heart, 'There is no God'" (Ps. 14:1, NIV).

The Alien

Time people are a carbon-based life-form that have basically declared themselves extant through their sentient self-awareness. They actually think that time began before they themselves did. Almost unanimously, they have adopted the notion that they are occupying only a momentary segment in the infinitesimal string of time.

But this position is a result of their own deliberate choice and nothing more. Unfortunately for them, there is no real need for their misunderstanding of their existence and significance in the cosmic reckoning.

The time people inhabit a so-called green planet spinning gently in a small orbit around a dim star in an out-of-the-way pocket of a galaxy in the celestial wasteland. The green designation indicates that their home world sustains organic qualities that set it apart from the mere gases and minerals that comprise the rest of the known universe.

The expression "known universe" brings an intriguing question to mind. One could easily ask, "Known by whom?"

But time people answer, "By us, of course. Who else is there?"

They measure everything against themselves. What the known universe means to the time people, really, is that they *know* that the universe exists, that they live like a mote in a moonbeam—yet they know almost nothing about the rest of the infinite cosmos.

They merely wonder, *How could we ever expect to understand our place in the universe if we don't understand ourselves?* What they don't realize is that if they can truly answer either of these questions, they will have answered them both.

And a curious thing is that the answer came to them once, appeared from seemingly nowhere right in their midst, but they didn't recognize it for what it was. There it stood among them, breathing, eating, sleeping, weeping. In so many ways it looked so much like they themselves, yet it acted so *alien* that they couldn't accept it.

The answer wasn't of the kind that comes as a sudden, piercing insight. Neither was it a quiet, dawning realization. Both of these come from within, and that is where the time people are used to looking for answers to their greatest questions. If they're concerned at all about these issues, and amazingly few of them are, they spend a great deal of mental effort obsessing over their own essence.

Instead the answer came from without. This was a concept that simply didn't compute in their thinking. And it made them very uncomfortable.

They are a race that does not like discomfort of any kind. In fact, they resent it. *If I indeed exist and know I exist,* they reason, *then I must be pretty important, and I am the best judge of what is best for me. I determine what is truth. Whatever answers I need will surely come from deep inside me.*

So the time people decided that the answer didn't solve their questions at all. It was just too simple yet too alien, and it came from the wrong place.

Well, this is not entirely true. A few—a very few—of them caught a vision of the impossible. They realized that even though the alien answer didn't come from within them, it could be *allowed* into them to become a part of them, if they were willing to accept such an arrangement. As it happens, the time people have the ability to accept the ultimate answer to their existence when it comes to them, but virtually all of them choose not to.

Part of the problem of accepting this arrangement is that the home world of the time people is the only one they have ever known. Throughout their history they've been butting their heads against their own self-imposed limitations.

Some actually express the wish that if they could only glimpse this alien superuniverse that exists outside their own experience, just once see some clear empirical proof of it, then they would gladly embrace the answer. With that goal in mind, they conduct research, build machines, write treatises, found institutes, formulate philosophies, explore frontiers, exchange information, convene conferences . . .

Yet the interesting thing is that the few who have caught the vision of this alien superuniverse are already in it. They haven't actually left at all, but they're already there.

They have accepted the truth that they can be inside time and outside time—at the same time!

➤ Consider this sentence: "The few who have caught the vision of this alien superuniverse are already in it." How does this statement agree or disagree with what you have read in the previous chapter's readings on the kingdom of heaven?

➤ A frequent theme of motion pictures and television shows is: The truth is in you. What does Scripture say about this approach to truth?

➤ Read John 14:6 in several translations. Meditate on the meaning of this text as it relates to humankind's search for truth.

Day 2

"Let not the wise man boast of his wisdom" (Jer. 9:23, NIV).

Philosophy 101 Final Exam

Did we derive from some
    infinity of nonintent?
Are we culmination
    of a cosmic accident?
Do we trace our lineage

up or down—

are we a ladder rung

or spring growth on a dying tree

or merely locus on a spiral line?

Are we diamonds in the rough,

or roughage in the diamonds?

Are we going anywhere,

or have we just arrived?

Is there anywhere, indeed, to go?

And if there is,

how will we know

when we've arrived?

Your answer will be graded

not in the logic

of your arguments—

preponderance of evidence—

but simply where you choose to plant

the weight of both your feet.

➤ On what does a wise person, boasting of their wisdom, "plant the weight" of their feet?

➤ What is the difference, if any, between knowledge and wisdom?

➤ Using a concordance, read carefully at least 10 references in the book of Proverbs that deal with wisdom. Then, in a single sentence, write your own definition of the word.

Day 3

"The human heart is . . . desperately wicked" (Jer. 17:9, NLT).

What's Mine Is Mine!

Pennsylvania State University sociologist Barry Ruback has recently offered the following interesting insights into our human nature:

- It takes an average of 27 seconds for a car to vacate a parking space if no one is waiting; if someone is waiting, it takes 31 seconds.

- The average call from a public telephone is 82 seconds if no one is waiting to use the phone; if someone is waiting, it takes four minutes.

Surprised? Probably not. Who hasn't suspected as much?

But what exactly is going on here? One explanation offered by sociologists is that this unwillingness to give up possession of something is a manifestation of our territorial instincts that go back millions of years. They say that it reflects a time in our evolution when such behavior was necessary for survival: "This cave is mine. Go find your own!"

When you think about it, however, it doesn't seem all that necessary to trace basic human selfishness back to cave dwellers. The fact is, humankind is just plain ornery. You see it every day in the me-first and what's-mine-is-mine attitudes that we display to one another. Humorist Garrison Keillor said it characteristically well in a monologue delivered at Carnegie Hall: "We're just plain rotten!"

The Bible says as much, too: "The human heart is . . . desperately wicked" (Jer. 17:9, NLT). But the Bible also offers the only solution to such all-too-human behavior: "O Lord, you alone can heal me; you alone can save. My praises are for you alone!" (verse 14, NLT).

Even though we're all sinful beings, however, often we aren't consciously treating others unkindly. We aren't deliberately being selfish; it's just that being human, we're considering only our own wishes and needs.

So next time you're using a public phone, remember to cut it short. God will be only too happy to help you do it!

➤ To what extent is being inconsiderate of others a result of pride?

➤ What evidences in your own life betray the human proneness to be inconsiderate of others?

➤ List three or four specific ways you can change your behavior to become more considerate of others. Think about why you should do so.

DAY 4

"Whoever wants to become great among you must be your servant, and whoever wants to be first must be your slave" (Matt. 20:26, 27, NIV).

THE RICH YOUNG RULER

"Well, I'll tell you," he said,
"I had a chance to talk
to Him myself one day—
ask Him how His philosophy
differs from our own.
'What must I do to be saved?'
I asked Him.
    "'Keep the commandments,' He said.
Can you imagine His telling me that?
Who keeps the commandments
better than we do?
To tell you the truth,

I'm not sure His own disciples
pay much attention to the law—
certainly less than they should.
I've heard they husk grain
and heal the sick on the Sabbath."

    The young ruler shook his head
and traced a slender finger
along the brocade of his robe.
"Then He said to me,
'Give your possessions to the poor!'
Now, I ask you where He got that
from the commandments.
Since when is it a sin
to have a little money?
I've worked hard for mine.

    "If only He didn't openly contradict
so much of what we've been taught
since we were children.
After thousands of years
of refining our tradition,
He calls us white sepulchers.
Are we God's chosen,
or are we not?"

➤ To what extent is being "God's chosen" a great responsibility?

➤ Is tradition sinful? Explain your answer.

➤ Take an informal poll among at least six of your friends and/or family. Ask them this question: What church tradition do you think is the most valid?

DAY 5

"Do not put the Lord your God to the test" (Matt. 4:7, NIV).

THROW YOURSELF DOWN

Thor Axel Kappfjell was at the top of his sport—literally. As a member of the worldwide BASE organization, he liked to jump off tall things; BASE stands for buildings, antennas, spans (bridges), and earth (cliffs). BASE jumping is parachuting from fixed objects. Fun, huh?

Thor had gained quite a bit of notoriety around the world by jumping off things without permission. He leaped off the eighty-sixth-floor observation deck of the Empire State Building in New York City and, three days later, the eagle heads on the Chrysler Building.

Authorities cried, "Hey, you can't do that!" But both times the adventurer melted into the crowds of the teeming city before anyone could nab him. When he jumped from one of the World Trade towers, however, they were ready for him. He was arrested and sentenced to seven days of community service.

Then in July 1999, Thor was the third of 12 jumpers planning to leap from the 3,300-foot Kjerag, a cliff near Stavanger, Norway. It was Thor's last jump: he hit the rock face and fell into a fjord.

When Jesus was on earth He was faced at one time with the possibility of becoming human history's first known BASE jumper. Rather than getting His name into the pages of the *Guinness Book of World Records,* however, His experience is reported in Scripture. When you think about it, the New Testament is far more amazing than *Guinness,* anyway! How can such things as the world's longest mustache or the most jumps recorded on a pogo stick or the largest tomato ever compare to the miracle of Jesus Christ?

Jesus' opportunity to become the world's first BASE jumper occurred when He was confronted in the wilderness by Satan. The devil threw three pitches at Him, hoping that these fastballs would be enough to strike Him out once and for all.

In the second temptation, while Jesus was at the top of the Temple, Satan suggested, "Throw yourself down" (Matt. 4:6, NIV). To some that may sound like fun, but of course doing it simply for the thrill of it wasn't the point. Jesus saw clearly what was implied.

We're assured elsewhere that Jesus "has been tempted in every way, just as we are" (Heb. 4:15, NIV). Not too many of us, however, have been tempted to become literal BASE jumpers. So how does Jesus' temptation at the top of the Temple conform to the idea that He was "tempted in every way, just as we are"? How did that experience present a problem that is universal to the rest of humankind?

Jesus Himself provided the answer: the point wasn't adventuring, but presumption. Most dictionary definitions of "presumption" usually include such synonyms as arrogance, audacity, pride, temerity, or effrontery.

Though presumption seldom appears as such in various translations of Scripture, it describes a form of sin that recurs rather regularly. We see it in an arrogant idea that a tower would protect humankind from a future flood; in Jonah's audacity to question God's mercy in sparing the people of Nineveh; in the temerity of Jesus' brothers counseling *Him* that "no one who wants to become a public figure acts in secret" (John 7:4, NIV). Presumption simply means putting oneself in God's place, forgetting one's dependence on Him.

In Jesus' temptation experience, Satan actually quoted from Scripture. Daring Jesus to throw Himself off the pinnacle of the Temple, Satan reminded Him with wicked cunning, "It is written: 'He will command his angels concerning you, and they will lift you up in their hands, so that you will not strike your foot against a stone'"(Matt. 4:6, NIV).

When Satan quoted Scripture, however, he chose not to include a crucially important part: "to guard you in all your ways" (Ps. 91:11, NIV). If Jesus had followed this suggestion, He would have been venturing into Satan's ways, not the ways that God intended for Him.

Every temptation that comes our way is rooted in the idea that we don't have to take God at His word. It shows a distrust in God and in His revelation in Scripture.

God's power is not something that we can experiment with. It is a force that we're expected to trust quietly in our everyday lives. This is why Jesus answered Satan's second pitch by referring to the book of Deuteronomy: "It is also written: 'Do not put the Lord your God to the test'" (Matt. 4:7, NIV).

In Jesus' answer we can begin to see how universal this temptation is. Who among us can say we've never stretched God's protection for us a bit too far? Who can claim that we are *always* totally dependent on God in *everything* we do?

- Consider your own life over the past year. In what ways have you "put the Lord your God to the test"?

- How can a Christian know which risks are appropriate and which are presumptuous?

- In prayer, ask God to reveal to you clearly the ways in which you have put Him to the test. Spend some quiet time actually listening for an answer to this question.

Day 6

"Do not deceive yourselves. If any one of you thinks he is wise by the standards of this age, he should become a 'fool' so that he may become wise" (1 Cor. 3:18, NIV).

THE GREAT CYCLE CONTROVERSY

Once there was a kid
who had the shiniest bicycle on the block—
chrome fenders, flashing reflectors, glittering paint—
and every other kid in the neighborhood
did his best to make his bike just like Lucky's.

CLICK HERE

They gathered on his front lawn
and talked about bicycles
and polished their fenders with soft cloth
and read detailed articles in *Cycling Review*
about the finer points of owning a bike.

Then a new kid moved into the neighborhood—
Michael was his name—
and, of course, everyone wanted to see his bicycle.
It was mere tires and tubing—
no glitter; no shine; no flash!
He suggested quietly that bikes, after all,
were more for riding than polishing—
that they were made to go places.

But Lucky wouldn't let him join the group,
and although one or two sided with Michael,
most of the kids seemed content merely
to polish their fenders with soft cloth.

➤ In what ways did Lucky's friends think Michael was a fool?

➤ What is the relationship, if any, between pride and foolishness? Explain your answer.

➤ Write a personal experience in which you learned a lesson
about pride. Submit it to *Insight* magazine for publication.

Day 7

"If anyone thinks he is something when he is nothing, he deceives himself" (Gal. 6:3, NIV).

Making It Personal

Try some of the following activities as you complete this week's consideration of the subject of pride:

- From a dictionary of thoughts or quotations, look up several definitions for the word "pride." Then, using a concordance, compare these definitions to what the Bible says about pride.

- Imagine yourself a TV interviewer transported back to the time of Solomon. Using quotations from the book of Proverbs, write an interview in which you ask Solomon, the wisest person who ever lived, how someone with so much wisdom could be overcome with pride.

- From clay, plaster, wood, or other medium, sculpt something that illustrates the destructive nature of human pride.

- Explore some of the dynimations at this URL: http://www.heartlight.org/dynimation. See if you can find one or two that illustrate pride, and send them to some of your friends who you think may appreciate them.

- Listen to Wayne Watson's contemporary Christian song "The Urgency (of the Generally Insignificant)." Think about the way in which pride makes you focus on insignificant things when you should be focusing on Jesus.

9

DAY 1:

"Do not conform any longer to the pattern of this world, but be transformed by the renewing of your mind. Then you will be able to test and approve what God's will is—his good, pleasing and perfect will" (Rom. 12:2, NIV).

MONKEYING AROUND WITH THE WORLD

Officials at Washington's National Zoo thought that it was time to give their rare golden lion tamarins an area to live in that was more like their natural habitat. So the officials designed the zoo-raised monkeys' new living quarters to simulate as nearly as possible the lowland Brazilian forest from which the species had come.

This, however, created an unexpected problem for the zookeepers. When the cage-raised monkeys were first introduced to their new, more open and natural living area, they showed that they had lost many of the basic skills for their species. They fell out of the trees, and one of them even got lost in the woods.

The importance of environment in life is as influential to Christians as it is to other members of the animal kingdom. This is why Paul warned Christians not to conform "to the pattern of this world." In too many ways the pattern of this world runs counter to what the Bible tells us is for our best. What we read, what we watch, what we listen to—all these influences have an impact on how we live out our Christian lives.

Paul knew how much the influences of the world can have an effect on the everyday life of Christians and cause them to lose the "basic skills" of Christianity. It's much more important, he says, to be able to "test and approve what God's will is" (Rom. 12:2, NIV).

➤ The tamarins in the National Zoo became less like tamarins because of their limited environment. In our world, however, we can become less like humans because of our unlimited environment. How should we go about limiting our environment for our own safety from worldliness? Be specific.

➤ In what ways do you feel "caged" by the world?

➤ Visit a zoo and observe the way in which animals are caged. Think about the impact this has on their natural behaviors, and on how this may have lessons for overcoming worldliness.

DAY 2

"Set your minds on things above, not on earthly things" (Col. 3:2, NIV).

BALAAM

The road that he had chosen

lay dream-dust warm before him.

All along the way

the golden carrot lured him on.

Imagine the embarrassment:

a donkey's sight—

and speech—

were truer than the prophet's.

➤ In what ways was Balaam's mistake similar to those of the tamarins (see Day 1)?

CLICK HERE

➤ In practical terms, how can one keep his or her mind focused on "things above"?

➤ Copy today's text (Col. 3:2) on an index card and place it where it will serve as a reminder to focus on "things above."

Day 3

"Remain in me, and I will remain in you. No branch can bear fruit by itself, it must remain in the vine. Neither can you bear fruit unless you remain in me" (John 15:4, NIV).

THE INTERCONNECTIONS OF LIFE

Until recently scientists have thought of trees as relatively insensitive green machines that furnish oxygen for our environment and wood for our homes. But recent research indicates that these green machines seem to communicate and even cooperate with each other, and they are influenced distinctly by their environment.

In the early 1980s a chemical ecologist at the University of Washington at Seattle discovered that when willows are attacked by webworms and tent caterpillars, they give off a chemical alarm that alerts other nearby willows of the threat. When this happens, the neighboring trees begin to produce a substance that will make them more resistant to the attack of the insects.

Furthermore, a researcher at Oregon State University found that when the roots of neighboring trees touch, the natural competition between them is sometimes overridden by a fungus that can actually link the roots together. This helps to develop a network among the roots that makes it possible for one tree to pass nutrients to its weaker neighbor. "Thanks to these fungi," says the researcher, "it could be that a whole forest is linked together like a community. If one tree has access to water, another to nutrients, a third to sunlight, the trees apparently can share with one another."

The world around us certainly has an impact on us, both positive and negative. God has provided a great many blessings for us through our surroundings. Yet the world has become under the influence of Satan, and that means that we can be impacted negatively as well.

As we face life's problems and challenges, it is a source of great encouragement to know that Jesus is always available to us. We can look to Him for strength and support as surely as the trees rely on each other for growth and nourishment—even in a sometimes hostile environment.

- How are the mutual defenses formed by the trees similar to and different from the defenses we can form in relationship with Jesus?

- What connections do you have with those around you that may be positive or negative?

- Take a walk through a forest or go to a place where you can observe some trees. Think about the ways in which trees defend themselves and how this may be applied to your own life.

DAY 4

"Unless you change and become like little children, you will never enter the kingdom of heaven" (Matt. 18:3, NIV).

A SMALL MISUNDERSTANDING

Once there was a little girl
who misunderstood the question
the teacher asked in class—
"What do you want to be
when you grow up?"

She said she wanted to be an angel.

The rest of the kids

laughed and grinned and elbowed one another;

it was the kind of thing

they'd learned to expect of her.

She was embarrassed—

but she shouldn't have been.

➤ How does the little girl in "A Small Misunderstanding" illustrate the meaning of Matthew 18:3?

➤ Why do you think the girl who wanted to be an angel shouldn't have been embarrassed?

➤ List five things you should do in your own life that would help you to "become like little children."

DAY 5

"He who has ears to hear, let him hear!" (Matt. 13:9, NKJV).

LISTEN UP!

The noise of human activity in the earth's oceans is beginning to concern scientists, because it seems to be harming sea life. The nearly extinct bowhead whale will go almost six miles out of its way on its migration route to avoid a drilling ship. Narwhals and belugas—two species of arctic whales—have been found to be very sensitive to the noise of ice-breaking ships. Belugas make alarm calls when the ships are still as far as 50 miles away.

According to studies at the University of Miami, marine animals have a keen sense of hearing. In addition to using it as a form of communication, many depend on sound to navigate in depths where they can't see. Underwater blasting and drilling can damage the hearing organs of fish and mammals. It can also slow the growth rates and damage the eggs of fish, reducing the catch of commercial fishermen.

The human sense of hearing is not as acute as that of others of God's creatures. But we were created with an adequate ability to hear, and God expects us to use all our senses to the best of our abilities. However, when Jesus said, "Who has ears to hear, let him hear," He wasn't really speaking about our sense of hearing. What He really meant was, "Listen up! This is important, and I want you to understand it fully. It's for your own good."

There is a great deal of spiritual noise going on in the world around us. And if we're not careful of our spiritual sense of hearing, we can become deafened by it.

If the beluga whale can hear danger as far as 50 miles away, you'd think we could at least learn to avoid some of the dangers that Satan puts in our path. And we should always be thankful that God has provided us with ears and a brain so we can hear and understand the wonderful truths He has given us.

➤ What kinds of "spiritual noise" appear to have the greatest impact on your life?

➤ How do you know whether spiritual noise is positive or negative?

➤ For one hour, put a piece of cotton in each ear, blotting all noise out. Use this time to concentrate on communicating with God and His communicating with you.

DAY 6

"Look at the birds of the air; they do not sow or reap or store away in barns, and yet your heavenly Father feeds them. Are you not much more valuable than they?" (Matt. 6:26, NIV).

MIND-MAKERS

Subtle whispers

in the unconscious ear,

creating appetites

for throwaways

and substitutes—

gilded promises

of supersexuality,

when nothing else matters

and you'd kill for it—

a lie through smiling teeth.

➤ How would you define "Mind-makers" as they are described in this poem?

➤ What is the "lie through smiling teeth"?

➤ Look through magazines or newspapers to find examples of what you think is meant by the "lie through smiling teeth."

DAY 7

"Still others, like seed sown among thorns, hear the word; but the worries of this life, the deceitfulness of wealth and the desires for other things come in and choke the word, making it unfruitful" (Mark 4:18, 19, NIV).

MAKING IT PERSONAL

Try some of the following activities as you complete this week's consideration of the subject of worldliness:

- For a week keep a journal in which you carefully record your activities each day and the time spent on each activity. At the end of the week, consider what each activity suggests about your dealing with worldliness.

- Most devotional books—those organized with a day-by-day reading for a year—contain an index of the scriptural references featured in the readings. From devotional books that you may have on hand, read some of the passages that refer to the scriptural references in this week's readings on the subject of worldliness.

- Select one of the scriptural references from this week's readings and feature it in a computer design for a small poster. Experiment with fonts, borders, images, textures, etc. Place the poster where it can serve as a reminder of the importance of overcoming worldliness.

- Think of three examples of worldliness as it is illustrated in object lessons from nature. Prepare to share one of these examples in a short presentation for children.

- Explore your own home, and list the things you see in it that could serve to encourage worldliness in your life. Think about what you should do to avoid these influences.

10

Day 1

"A gentle answer turns away wrath, but a harsh word stirs up anger" (Prov. 15:1, NIV).

What Gets Your Goat?

There is an old tradition that to soothe high-strung thoroughbred horses, trainers would often put a companion animal in their stalls. Goats were among the most frequent kind of animal used for this kind of thing, and the horses often became very attached to their stablemates.

Sometimes, however, a trainer from a rival barn would sneak into a horse stall the night before a race and kidnap a goat in an attempt to upset the horse and thereby cause it to run a poor race the next day.

Language experts have suggested that this practice was the source of the expression "gets my goat," to mean something that makes someone angry or upset. Whatever it is that gets your goat—that makes you angry—King Solomon provided some effective advice: "A gentle answer turns away wrath, but a harsh word stirs up anger."

One of the best ways to avoid becoming angry over something someone has said to you is simply to ignore it. After someone once insulted Buddha, he asked, "Son, if someone declined to accept a present, to whom would it belong?"

The man responded, "To him who offered it."

"And so," said Buddha, "I decline to accept your abuse."

And this is exactly what happens when you refuse to accept the insults of others. It returns to them.

🡖 What kinds of things make you angry? What specifically can you do about it?

🡖 How can you apply the principle of a "soft answer"?

🡖 In prayer, ask God to help you develop specific strategies to cope with the things in life that make you angry.

DAY 2

"Live in harmony with one another" (Rom. 12:16, NIV).

HUE AND CRY

Once there was a congregation
who couldn't agree on what color
to paint their church.
Some wanted it red,
symbolic of the blood the Savior shed.
Others preferred springlike green,
a reminder of Christ's resurrection.
And others wanted white—
purity, Christ's robe, angels' wings.
Committee meetings lasted long into the night;
members traded charges, countercharges, insults.
After the nineteenth ballot
they decided to table the issue indefinitely.
"If we can't have it white," someone muttered,
"then we won't paint it at all!"
And the church,

unprotected against the elements—

the real reason for the paint, after all—

decomposed like a corpse.

➤ Is it possible to be angry and live in harmony? Explain your answer.

➤ What is the difference, if any, between anger and stubbornness?

➤ List five times that Jesus appeared not to be in harmony with those around Him. Analyze these situations, and write three principles for when harmony should be disrupted.

Day 3

"Do not be quickly provoked in your spirit" (Eccl. 7:9, NIV).

LIVING IN A POWDER KEG?

Spare time is not in Annie's vocabulary. She is a junior class officer with a 3.8 GPA, a Pathfinder counselor, a reader for one of the English teachers, and more. If you want something done right, you get Annie to do it. Ask anybody—except maybe Annie herself.

That's because she sometimes feels as though she can't stop to take a deep breath. She's up at 5:45 a.m., throws together a sack lunch for herself and her 9-year-old brother, and is at her desk in world history class by 7:45. The rest of the day is a blur, and weekends are little better. She looks in the mirror and wonders what is missing in her life. Like the words in the song, she feels as if she's "living in a powder keg and giving off sparks." And when things are like this, she finds it easy to become frustrated, irritable, angry.

Annie knows she should slow down, but she just doesn't have a clue as to how to go about it. She feels guilty every time she takes a few minutes for herself. *After all,* she thinks, *idleness is the devil's workshop. The Bible doesn't say a thing about relaxation.* Or does it?

Architect Frank Lloyd Wright once told of an experience in his life that had a lasting influence on him. At the age of 9 he went walking across a snow-covered field with his reserved, no-nonsense uncle. As the two of them reached the far end of the field, his uncle stopped him. He pointed out his own tracks in the snow, straight and true as an arrow's flight, and then young Frank's tracks wandering all over the field.

"Notice how aimless your tracks are—from the fence to the cattle to the woods and back again," his uncle said. "And see how my tracks aim directly to my goal. There is an important lesson in that."

Years later the world-famous architect liked to tell how this experience had greatly contributed to his philosophy in life. "I determined right then," he said with a twinkle in his eye, "not to miss most things in life—as my uncle had."

Unfortunately, some Christians make the same mistake as Frank Lloyd Wright's uncle. Like Annie, they are uncomfortable with relaxation and spontaneity.

Two of Jesus' best friends while He was on this earth—two sisters—were very different from each other. Martha went about life as directly as possible, without looking right or left. Mary's interest was easily aroused by the world around her. If the two sisters had walked across the same field as Frank Lloyd Wright and his uncle, Martha's tracks would have been straight; Mary's would have wandered.

And Jesus actually defended Mary's simple, honest reaction to things that were going on around her. "'Martha, Martha,' the Lord answered, 'you are worried and upset about many things, but only one thing is needed. Mary has chosen what is better, and it will not be taken away from her'" (Luke 10:41, 42, NIV).

Most New Testament Christians were intense, no-nonsense people, and, of course, when you have a world to win, you can get pretty caught up in your work. But by defending Mary, Jesus suggested there are also appropriate times for the simple wonder that is aroused by God's amazing gifts to us.

➤ What can Annie do in practical terms to avoid becoming provoked?

➤ In what areas of your life do you think you should learn to slow down?

➤ Draw an imaginary field of snow in which you sketch the direction that your life is taking—is it straight or meandering? Why?

DAY 4

"Seek peace and pursue it" (Ps. 34:14, NIV).

THE ZEALOT

Simon had something to say,
something that simply wouldn't stay
safely sheathed in care or tact.
It wasn't his way
to keep his feelings to himself—
never had been.
His anger had always been
the focus of his life.
He thrust a finger into Levi Matthew's chest
and squinted straight into his eyes.
"A word with you, if I may"—
less question than demand.
    Right from the very beginning
this confrontation had been foreseen.
Someone had put it well:

"Can fire and water coexist?"
      Levi Matthew, apprehensive,
faltered back a step or two.
Until now he'd managed to evade
direct connection with the zealot,
stayed out of Simon's way.
It was a role he'd learned so well
in working as he had for Rome.
      Simon only smiled,
but Matthew was experienced enough
to know that smiles sometimes sting.
Was it an arming or disarming smile?
      "I thought it best to say this
while the Master is away," Simon began.
"There's something that I think
you need to hear from me—directly.
When I responded to His invitation,
it looked as if at last
here was a way to lance the boil
that is Rome.
It was as clear to me as brightest day
that someone of your ilk would have to go,
and I was just the man to help you on your way.
You'll never know how many times
I've had my knifepoint at your back,
prepared to weed you out,
a tare among the wheat.
After all, if we're to throw off the yoke of Rome,

how can we abide the kind
who've betrayed our people as you have?"

His eyebrows furrowed into deeper thought.
"But something always made me wait;
I don't know how I can account for that.
Waiting's new to me, you know.
I've never bothered to put off
what clearly needed to be done."

The words came one by one,
as if each must bear the pain of birth itself.
"What all this means is this:
we are of one heart now, you and I,
though how that came to be
is a mystery I shall never fully understand."

He stopped, at a loss to express a thought
as amazing to himself
as it could ever be to anyone else:
"You have no more to fear from me."

➤ How did Simon the zealot "seek peace"?

➤ What changes in your life should you make to seek peace?

➤ Think about someone you know with whom you should seek peace. Get in touch with him or her (e-mail, note, telephone, face-to-face), and see what you can do to put an end to your differences.

DAY 5

"Have you any right to be angry?" (Jonah 4:4, NIV).

THE DROPOUT PROPHET

At the 1960 Portland (Oregon) City Amateur Golf Tournament, a young golfer named Kelly Stroud teed off on the three-par sixteenth hole and, with a sinking heart, watched the ball plop into the water. So Kelly took his penalty and teed off again—right into the water. His third shot went the same way. But Kelly wasn't a quitter. His fourth shot flew a perfect 148 yards straight into the cup for a four-over-par hole in one.

Fortunately, Kelly Stroud didn't quit after his first three shots the way the prophet Jonah did when God spared Nineveh. In some ways Jonah's reaction was understandable. After all, if you're a prophet of God and you predict that God is going to wipe out a whole city, you're really going out on a limb with everybody watching. One of the ways that people judge their prophets is by how well their predictions come true. Jonah thought that his reputation was at stake. So when God decided to spare Nineveh, Jonah felt like dropping out of the tournament. "This game isn't for me!" he said to God.

But God just asked Jonah what he was so angry about. He pointed out that in serving Him there are other considerations besides reputation. In this case it was the lives of more than 120,000 people.

What's important is staying in the game and doing what God has given you to do. Failure and success are best measured on God's scorecard, and if we just keep trying, He will give us each a hole in one.

➤ When, if ever, is it appropriate to be angry?

➤ When is it appropriate to keep trying, and when is it appropriate to quit?

➤ Many Bible commentators consider that Jesus showed anger when He cleansed the Temple. Read about it in John 2:13-

16. Based on this event, do you think Jesus was angry? If so, what principles can you establish to show when anger may be appropriate.

DAY 6

"One given to anger stirs up strife, and the hothead causes much transgression" (Prov. 29:22, NRSV).

ENOUGH IS ENOUGH!

For a while there Christakis Karamanos was receiving 300 wrong-number telephone calls a day. It seems his number was very close to that of the state radio headquarters of Cyprus, and Greek Cypriots were calling because they wanted to air their viewpoints on a talk show.

Karamanos contacted the telephone company and asked to have his number changed, but the bureaucrats at the company just didn't see the need.

Finally, after listening to his phone ring off the hook day and night for months, Karamanos, a demolition contractor, just snapped. He revved up his bulldozer, flattened the front gate of the Cyprus Broadcasting Corporation, and headed for the newsroom. Security guards hurriedly summoned the riot police. Two officers leaped up onto the bulldozer and brought it to a stop—a mere matter of feet from the building.

Probably most of us can sympathize with Karamanos. In his place we'd probably be tempted to do something similar. Everybody has a limit, and everybody "flies off the handle" now and again. But losing your temper almost always leads to destructive results. That's what Solomon meant when he wrote that angry people stir up strife and transgression. Although it may be a very human failing, it just isn't God's way of finding solutions.

▶ What alternatives can you think of that would have helped Christakis Karamanos find a solution to his problem?

➤ What experiences have you had that are similar to Karamanos's?

➤ Browse through a daily newspaper, and analyze how many of the articles relate to anger.

DAY 7

"When the ways of people please the Lord, he makes even their enemies live at peace with them" (Prov. 16:7, NLT).

MAKING IT PERSONAL

Try some of the following activities as you complete this week's consideration of the subject of anger:

➤ From a dictionary of thoughts or quotations, look up several quotations regarding the words "anger" and "angry." Copy your favorite quotation on a bookmark for your own future use.

➤ Imagine yourself a TV news reporter transported back to Jesus' time. Write an imaginary interview with several witnesses to Jesus' cleansing of the Temple (John 2:13-16). Ask and answer such questions as: Why do you think Jesus committed this act? Did He appear to be out of control? What do you think will be the result of this event? Etc.

➤ Phone a friend, and ask how he or she deals with frustration and anger. Between the two of you, outline several strategies for overcoming this problem.

➤ Create a puppet show in which you discuss and demonstrate ways to overcome anger. Perform the puppet show for a children's group.

CLICK HERE

➷ On the Internet, explore the relationship between anger and physical illness. What unhealthful changes occur in the body of someone who is angry?

11

DAY 1

"To every thing there is a season, and a time to every purpose under the heaven" (Eccl. 3:1).

KEEPING YOUR EYE ON THE BALL

Because they played for teams in different leagues, baseball greats Henry Aaron and Yogi Berra had little opportunity to play against each other. In the 1957 World Series, however, the New York Yankees, for whom Berra played catcher, were matched against the Milwaukee Braves, for whom Aaron played right field.

On one occasion Henry Aaron came to the plate to face the Yankee pitcher. Berra, who was catching, noticed that the Braves' right fielder was holding his bat in an unusual way. "Turn the bat around in your hands," Berra suggested, "so you can see the trademark."

"Didn't come up here to read," Aaron said without taking his eyes off the pitcher's mound. "Came up here to hit!"

Early in his life Henry Aaron had learned the valuable lesson that he should concentrate on whatever he was doing and that there are times when certain things are appropriate and others are inappropriate.

Too often distractions cause lack of concentration—even in spiritual matters. If we aren't careful, the little things in life can distract us from the big, important things. It's awfully easy to overlook such important things as prayer when we're harried by the petty responsibilities of everyday life.

For Henry Aaron, the most important thing when he was standing in the batter's box was to be prepared for the pitch. That kind of preparedness helped him become one of the greatest home-run hitters of all time. If we keep our eye on the ball, if we continue our connection to God through prayer, we can be just as successful in our spiritual life.

➤ How is prayer like keeping your eye on the ball?

➤ On a scale of 1 to 10 (1 = never; 10 = constantly), how well do you stay connected to God through prayer?

➤ Watch a sporting event on TV, and think about the importance that the athletes place on focus. How important does it appear to be to maintain constant focus on the game?

DAY 2

"I have sought your face with all my heart; be gracious to me according to your promise" (Ps. 119:58, NIV).

A PRAYER

I can't seem

to stuff my life

into the trim little boxes

that everyone else has

(if I'm to judge

by *Good Housekeeping*

and O. Henry stories

and reruns of *Happy Days*).

The step-by-step how-to articles

and self-appraisals

just don't produce

the gratifying denouement

that they're supposed to

at the end of the day.

Please, Lord,

rewrite my script,

and I'll stop improvising.

➤ How does asking God to "be gracious" relate to the request for Him to "rewrite my script"?

➤ In what specific ways do you need to ask God to rewrite your script?

➤ Interview someone in your congregation who has an especially rich prayer life. Ask him or her how to go about connecting with God in more meaningful ways.

DAY 3

"I lift up my voice to the Lord for mercy. I pour out my complaint before him; before him I tell my trouble" (Ps. 142:1, 2, NIV).

A FUELISH MISTAKE

On January 25, 1990, Avianca Airlines Flight 52 ran out of fuel and crashed to the earth, causing the loss of many lives. In its report of the incident, the U.S. National Transportation Safety Board discovered that the whole tragic accident may have been prevented if the flight crew had used the correct terms to describe their problem.

Reportedly, the pilots had radioed this message to the air traffic controllers: "We're running out of fuel."

In fact, the pilots used the wrong terms. If the crew had described their situation as having "minimum fuel" or "emergency fuel," as they were supposed to, the air traffic controllers would have known to respond decisively and immediately. Those were the terms they were trained to be listening for, but because they didn't hear them, they did not know the gravity of the situation.

Fortunately, when you send out a message to God for help, you don't have to do so in specific language or forms. There is no "standard operating procedure" that everyone must follow in communicating with God. He is more than happy to respond to you anytime and anywhere if you approach Him for help, as any true friend would.

The words—and their meanings—are not nearly as important as what is in your heart. And if your heart is right, there are no limits to what God can do through and for you.

▲ If specific language isn't the most important consideration in the quality of prayer, what is?

▲ In everyday language, explain what is meant by the words "if your heart is right."

▲ Underline, highlight, or otherwise mark the scriptural references that appear at the beginning of each day's part of this week's readings. In your future Bible reading, watch for other examples of God's acceptance.

DAY 4

"The earnest prayer of a righteous person has great power and wonderful results" (James 5:16, NLT).

SUPER BOWL

The priests had won the toss,

    electing to receive;

a hush fell over

    the sellout crowd,

a bunch of fair-weather fans.
As the team broke from the huddle—
first and ten—
and executed all their plays
(unnecessary roughness),
they finally had to punt.
Couldn't gain a yard.

And then Elijah
consulted his playbook
and summoned the water boy—
an unexpected strategy.
A master of the vertical game,
Elijah struck with lightning speed—
threw the bomb.
And with that unorthodox style
he changed the face of the game
for years to come.

➤ How did Elijah's experience on Mount Carmel exemplify the meaning of James 5:16?

➤ How could the following images apply to the improvement of your personal prayer life: consulting the playbook; summoning the water boy; throwing the bomb? Be specific.

➤ Phone a friend who is a football fan, and read the poem "Super Bowl" to him or her. Discuss the ways in which the poem applies to negative and positive qualities in one's prayer life.

DAY 5

"Give ear to my words, O Lord, consider my sighing. Listen to my cry for help, my King and my God, for to you I pray" (Ps. 5:1, 2, NIV).

JUST GIVE A LITTLE WHISTLE

No need for telephones on Gomera, one of the seven inhabited Canary Islands. If a farmer wishes to communicate with a neighbor across the valley from him, he just whistles.

Among inhabitants of this island, each letter of the alphabet has a corresponding sound. As someone whistles out his message, it sounds exactly like the song of a bird. Those who practice this kind of communication—called *silbo*—say that in good weather they can hear each other for distances of up to two miles.

There are three components in any successful communication: a sender, a receiver, and a message coded in a language that both sender and receiver understand. If the wind is blowing in the wrong direction or the Gomera farmer's neighbor across the valley is deaf or doesn't understand the whistle signals, the farmer could be wasting his breath. When conditions are right, however, the farmer and his neighbor have perfected a way of communicating that is just as good as anything AT&T could offer.

That is the way it is with prayer. If God could not hear our prayers or understand the language in which we send them, we would be wasting our breath. But like the psalmist, we can know with confidence that God will listen to our "cry for help." And, unlike the farmer on Gomera, we will never have to worry about which way the wind is blowing.

➤ In what other ways could the practice of *silbo* be compared to prayer?

➤ In how many ways do you communicate with God?

⮢ Experiment with communicating with God through other ways besides speech. Hum a piece of praise music, whistle a familiar hymn or contemporary Christian tune, meditate silently, etc.

DAY 6

"Don't let us yield to temptation, but deliver us from the evil one" (Matt. 6:13, NLT).

HOSTAGE!

How many days I've been here
I no longer know the count;
it used to be I took some care
in marking ciphers on the wall—
as if in that there were some good.
But now the length of time
is hardly worth the mentioning,
except that it has been too long;
one day might just as well have been
a life or an eternity,
what with the cool brutality—
assaulted daily
by the crude and the obscene.

So I sometimes lose touch
with right and wrong—
a moment only, but long enough
to make me question who I am

and why I am.
And to make frustration worse,
I know He paid
the ransom long ago;
all that's left for my release
is the playing out of strategy
and grim negotiation.

I'm nothing more than pawn
on the chessboard in my captor's mind.
Bound and gagged,
then tantalized with freedom's taste,
only to be reeled back in again,
knowing that I'm still interned and
cannot do what I really want to do.
My captor likes to trifle with my mind,
to tell me I'm abandoned—no one cares.
I don't know which is worse—
the desolation or the wait.

But liberation's on the way.
And prayerfully I breathe the words,
"Even so, come . . ."

➤ How is temptation described in the experience of the hostage in the poem?

➤ How does the poem "Hostage!" describe life for a Christian on this sinful earth? Be specific.

☚ Find something in your room that may be holding you hostage, may be coming between you and God. Pray about what God expects you to do about it.

Day 7

"The Lord is near to all who call on him" (Ps. 145:18, NIV).

Making It Personal

Try some of the following activities as you complete this week's consideration of the subject of prayer:

☚ Look through some books of classic art in which people are portrayed in prayer. Think about the feelings that these works of art evoke in you about the role of prayer in a person's life.

☚ Read *Thoughts From the Mount of Blessing,* pages 86, 87; *Gospel Workers,* pages 254-258.

☚ Photograph several subjects from nature, and put them together into a photo essay that expresses the qualities and importance of prayer.

☚ Write an imaginary e-mail prayer to God in which you use as many emoticons as you appropriately can. Go to < http://www.ker95.com/chat101/html/emoticons.html > for the definitions of the most popular emoticons.

☚ With several friends, form a prayer group that will meet regularly, and pray for one another as you seek to overcome sin in your lives.

12

DAY 1

"To those who are being saved we are a life-giving perfume" (2 Cor. 2:16, NLT).

NASAL ENGAGEMENT

For some decidedly dark reason, whenever people get enough time to spend on themselves, they always come up with creative ways to waste effort and resources. It's in their basic nature.

One of the most obvious examples of this tendency is the world of fashion. What a man wears, how a woman combs her hair, what children are clamoring for in the market, how a teenager speaks and walks—so much of what we think and do results from the swirling currents we're swimming in.

And the world of fashion influences all five senses. Oddly enough, it even extends to the olfactory.

At one particularly pivotal point in history, the human sense of smell had been developed to such esoteric ends that it had become a veritable art form. Through the ages the world of personal fragrances had become so finely nuanced that no one trusted their own senses anymore.

A great deal of time and expense had been committed to finding one's signature scent, that which somehow expressed something absolutely inexpressible about a person. Men slapped copious quantities of Old Spice, Brut, Polo, and Aramis onto their faces to create an effect on others. Women considered that such fragrances as Norrell, Safari, Knowing, and Trésor enhanced their lives in subtle yet important ways.

Through generations of experimentation and refinement, producers of these fragrances developed an industry that gradually assumed a dictatorial role in such matters. Over time this industry began to inform the masses what smelled good and what didn't. It was as though the everyday person had completely surrendered his sense of smell, as though the nose in her face belonged to someone else. The so-called experts put their heads together and drew up an extremely complicated system to govern people's sense of smell.

Then one day a little-known company from a developing country introduced a completely new fragrance with some quietly audacious claims: "Until now, you've been wearing the wrong fragrance," the straightforward advertising stated flatly. "Try Heaven Scent, and it will change your life!"

The introduction of the new fragrance created a bit of a stir at first. It was marketed in a radically different way from that of other such fashion products. There was no big media blitz, no inflated introduction offers, no celebrity spokespersons.

The packaging was just as forthright. The bottle in which the new fragrance came was nothing remarkable at all—just a basic, no-nonsense clear glass bottle. There was no attempt to make the packaging appear to be anything other than a container for a fragrance. It offered no suggestive shapes, no provocative shades or colors, no clever labeling.

One merchandising problem was that the fragrance was difficult to classify. Was it masculine or feminine? Blue-collar or aristocratic? Simple or sophisticated? You simply couldn't answer any of these questions clearly. None of these labels seemed to apply. The advertising was basic but persistent: "Heaven Scent will change your life!"

Everyone who got the faintest whiff of the new fragrance reacted in a different way. A few were instantly captivated by it; some yawned and wondered what all the excitement was about; some were repulsed outright. Almost all merely left the interpretation of this new fragrance to a self-appointed panel of experts.

Those few whose lives truly were affected by the new fragrance soon began a loosely organized campaign to introduce Heaven Scent to anyone who would listen. They began to show up here and there in the marketplace. With bottle in hand, they approached anyone who would allow eye contact. "Would you like to try Heaven Scent?" they asked. "It will change your life!"

But the fact is, though most people weren't any too happy with the way their lives were going, they were just too busy or too cosmopolitan to take such simple claims seriously. Their olfactory senses were so hypersensitized, so jaded, so deadened that they failed to realize that Heaven Scent was the simple, sweet fragrance of life the way it was always meant to be.

➤ In practical terms, what is meant by the expression Heaven Scent in the parable "Nasal Engagement"?

➤ How can a Christian be a perfume to someone else?

➤ At a cosmetic counter in a department store, explore some fragrances intended for the gender opposite your own. Think about which fragrances appeal to you and why they do so. Which do not appeal to you and why?

DAY 2

"Let your good deeds shine out for all to see, so that everyone will praise your heavenly Father" (Matt. 5:16, NLT).

GLOWING OUTWARD

Once there was a church
    with a stained-glass crucifixion
        that vied with the preacher
        for the attention
        of the dwindling congregation.
The rays of the sun
    shot through the blue

and violet and crimson.
Multicolored patches
    warmed the hands and faces
    and seemed to pierce
            the very hearts
            of the congregation sitting there.
And they basked in it
and smiled at one another
    but dwindled on,
    until the day
            an energetic whippersnapper
            said the church's trouble
            was that the light
            flowed into the church all right,
            but that the church
            soaked up the light like a sponge.
            "What we need to do," he said,
            "is light up that window from *inside*—
            glow a bit ourselves—
                    so that people outside can see it."
So the congregation tried it.
    They lit the window up at night,
    and before too long
            the water bill for the baptistry doubled.

➤ If you "let your good deeds shine out," how can you be sure
  that God receives the praise? Be specific.

➤ If you were a window, what changes in your life would you

125

need to make so the light could come from inside?

➤ Place a candle or a small light in your window as a reminder of your role in reflecting God's light to those around you.

DAY 3

"Be on the alert, stand firm in the faith" (1 Cor. 16:13, NASB).

LOOK OUT FOR THE JUNK

Nicholas Johnson is probably the highest-paid junk man in the world, but he isn't your average sanitary engineer. Johnson is NASA's senior scientist for orbital debris. More than 8,600 objects larger than a softball are circling the earth, and the U.S. Space Surveillance Network—using cameras, radar, and telescopes—has given each of them a number and tracks them day and night.

The Network has to do this to prevent the space shuttle, space stations, and other operating satellites from being struck by flying objects. Even so, accidents occur: in 1986 a spent rocket exploded into nearly 500 trackable pieces, one of which struck a French satellite 10 years later at a speed faster than nine miles a second and sheared off a 10-foot section. A Hasselblad camera, which slipped out of the grasp of astronaut Michael Collins during a space walk, still circles the earth in its very own orbit.

And things are going to get a lot more crowded up there, thanks to our growing penchant for pagers and cellular phones and fax machines. A cooperative agency representing 135 organizations currently operates 27 space satellites; in 1997 a Washington, D.C.-based company sent up the first of its projected 66 satellites; an outfit in Dulles, Virginia, launched the first of 28 satellites; and a corporation bankrolled by Bill Gates and others are establishing fiber-optic quality telecommunications anywhere in the world by positioning a constellation of 288 satellites. The risks of collision are going to become higher than ever.

Whenever the space shuttle is in orbit, the pilot keeps the shuttle's least vulnerable side facing the direction from which the junk is coming.

This is how it is with temptation in a Christian's life. We can be sailing along in our own quiet little orbit and suddenly be blindsided by something coming out of nowhere. It's much to our advantage to be vigilant, to "be on the alert, stand firm in the faith" (1 Cor. 16:13, NASB).

➤ How is the environment for satellites like that for Christians?

➤ In practical everyday terms, what does it mean to a Christian to "be on the alert"?

➤ Research the subject of satellites to see what they do and how they function. Think of other ways in which Christians are like satellites.

Day 4

"See to it that no one takes you captive through hollow and deceptive philosophy, which depends on human tradition and the basic principles of this world rather than on Christ" (Col. 2:8, NIV).

The Seller of Doves

The silence in the empty Temple
ran an icy finger down his back.
He dodged from shadow to shadow
until he came to the place
where his table had been.
His cages were smashed and doves escaped.
Stooping over in the darkness,

he groped along the cobbled ground
for any coins
that may still be there.
        "So, you've come back too!"
A voice behind him
thrilled a surge of panic
through his stomach.
But he smiled sheepishly—
only another merchant like himself.
        "He made a proper mess   ·
of things, didn't He?" the other said.
"The authorities are going to hear about this.
I have some money coming.
What bothers me most, I think,
is the audacity of the Man,
rampaging through here
as if the place belonged to Him."
        The seller of doves
nodded his agreement.
"Someone has to be here," he said,
"to do what we do.
I suppose He thinks the animals
will just miraculously appear
like the ram to Abraham.
I'm not exactly getting wealthy
selling doves to peasants here—
the taxes eat the profits up.
        "Some say He will

overthrow the Romans,

but I think

He's about to overthrow everything.

If He has His way,

we've more to lose

than a day's sales."

➤ What "basic principles of this world" are referred to in "The Seller of Doves"?

➤ What kinds of things, if any, do you think Jesus would drive out of the church you attend?

➤ Read some of the responsive readings pertaining to Christian life in the *Seventh-day Adventist Hymnal* (numbers 784, 785, 786, 787, 788, 789, 790). Think about how these are reflected in your own personal experience.

DAY 5

"Love is patient, love is kind. It does not envy, it does not boast, it is not proud" (1 Cor. 13.4, NIV).

RETURNING THE FAVOR

In 1854 Ulysses S. Grant resigned his commission from the Army. Because he was penniless and a long way from his home in Ohio, he went to the West Point home of a friend, Simon Bolivar Buckner. Graciously Buckner gave Grant enough money to see him through his immediate problems.

Eight years later Grant was back in the Army again, this time as an officer for the United States Army in the Civil War. When he captured Fort Donelson, the commanding officer of the surrendering forces was his old friend Buckner, who had done him such a kindness.

"Grant never forgot an act of kindness," Buckner wrote later. "After my surrender, Grant followed me to my quarters, leaving behind his own officers celebrating the victory. There in the shadows, in that modest manner peculiar to Grant, he handed me his purse."

About 2,000 years ago Jesus performed for us the greatest act of kindness imaginable to humanity. He gave His life so we would be able to survive this life's terrible pain, sickness, and death. Because of His sacrifice, we need not suffer the natural results of our own sinfulness.

We can never, of course, expect to repay the debt we owe to Jesus. But we do have an obligation to show our gratitude to Him by being loving to others—even to our enemies. Whenever we do something to help, Jesus says, it is the same as if we'd done it for Jesus Himself. This is the reason that it is so important to be kind and loving Christians. It's just like returning a favor.

➤ How did U. S. Grant demonstrate what is said about love in 1 Corinthians 13:4?

➤ Why is it so easy to forget what Jesus did for us when we are hurt by others?

➤ Think of a time from the past when someone has done something kind to you. Return the favor by doing something similar to three other people you know.

DAY 6

"You also are among those who are called to belong to Jesus Christ" (Rom. 1:6, NIV).

WRONG NUMBER

Once there was a man
who thought he had a call

to the ministry,

but it was a wrong number.

He passed the tests all right:

studied the commentaries

and translated the Greek.

But passing the tests

won't get you through Tuesday—

or any other day

you weren't cut out for.

So he became a hod carrier,

and with a load of cement on his back

he delivered a more eloquent sermon

than any he'd tried in the pulpit.

➤ What does it mean to be "called to belong to Jesus Christ"?

➤ How can one know what he or she is being called to do for Jesus?

➤ Draw an illustration of someone who is delivering a sermon as a hod carrier—or any other form of physical labor.

DAY 7

"Blessed are the pure in heart, for they will see God" (Matt. 5:8, NIV).

MAKING IT PERSONAL
Try some of the following activities as you complete this week's consideration of the subject of Christian living:

➤ Interview an elderly Christian about the difference between

Christian living today versus Christian living when he or she was young. In an open-minded way, ask him or her to explain why things were done differently in the earlier era.

➤ List 10 physical objects that you would place in a time capsule to express Christian living in the twenty-first century.

➤ Think of three object lessons from nature that illustrate the importance of accepting others as they are.

➤ Begin to make your own computer database to include a variety of media that enrich your faith in God.

➤ Design a front cover for a magazine called *Christian Life*. Include in the design the nameplate *Christian Life*, art illustration, and titles of three articles that you think are most important in dealing with the topic of Christian living.

DAY 1

"A good name is more desirable than great riches; to be esteemed is better than silver or gold" (Prov. 22:1, NIV).

WHAT'S IN A NAME?

Ninety percent of Americans recognize "Louisville Slugger" as the trade name of a baseball bat—even if they have never been to a professional baseball game, never played in Little League, never cared much for the game at all. And over the years Louisville Slugger bats have become such a part of the game that about 7 out of 10 professional baseball players use them.

Turned on lathes in Louisville, Kentucky, almost all these famous bats are made of northern white ash trees from New York and Pennsylvania. Trees must be at least 60 feet tall before they are cut, and the lumber must season for more than six months before it is turned on lathes. Each tree yields about 60 bats. Pros in the major and minor leagues use up about 180,000 bats in a baseball season.

Solomon said that a good name is greatly to be valued—far more than wealth. "A good name is more desirable than great riches; to be esteemed is better than silver or gold" (Prov. 22:1, NIV). He wasn't saying it's good to be popular. He didn't mean we should be so concerned about what others think of us that we compromise what we know to be right. What Solomon meant is that there is sometimes quite a bit of difference between popularity and respect.

Nowadays marketers go to a great deal of effort and expense to find a suitable name for a new product such as an automobile. They pay researchers to survey public response to all kinds of names before they adopt something such as Saturn or Lexus or Bronco or Cherokee. They know how important a name can be. A well-chosen name may mean the difference between success and failure.

The Bible seems to place a lot of importance on names, too. We are told that Jesus knows each of us by name—as any good shepherd would know the individual names of his sheep. You may want to remind yourself of this the next time you feel you're "just another brick in the wall." In a society such as ours, you may sometimes get the feeling that you are defined only by Social Security number, area code, driver's license number, or zip code. But God knows you by *name*.

➤ Why would a good name be important to a Christian?

➤ What is the difference between pride (which is negative) and self-respect (which is positive)?

➤ Write down the names of as many automobiles as you can think of. Consider which of these you respond to most positively. Think about why this is so.

DAY 2

"Cleanse me with hyssop, and I will be clean; wash me, and I will be whiter than snow" (Ps. 51:7, NIV).

MY CLOSET

I've always kept
   this door securely locked.
Throughout the years
   the junk has piled up—
      collected dust.
I've been ashamed for anyone to see
   what it contains—

just treasured trash.
Although I tried a thousand times,
        I never seemed to have the will
                to do a proper job
                of cleaning it myself—
                too many things in there
                        I simply couldn't throw away.
I finally gave it up—
        gave Him the key and looked the other way
                (as if I were a frightened child
                who could not bear to watch
                        the needle pierce the skin);
He came and swept my closet out
        and left it cleaner
                than it's ever been—
                even on the darkest, topmost shelf.
I'm proud to show it to you now;
        it's become my favorite room in all the house
                for what it was and is—
                a closet made into a trophy room.

➤ What do you think is meant by "treasured trash"?

➤ Do you have any treasured trash in your life?

➤ In prayer, ask God to clean out the treasured trash in your life.

Day 3

"To the arrogant I say, 'Boast no more'" (Ps. 75:4, NIV).

CREDIT WHERE IT'S DUE

From a twelfth-century chronicle, the story has been told of Canute, the Danish king of England from 1016 to 1035. One day he grew so tired of the flattery of his courtiers that he ordered that his chair be taken to the seashore. There, before them all, he commanded the waves of the sea not to get him wet. Soon the advancing tide lapped over his feet and proved the true worth of human commands—even those of kings.

Human accomplishment is a tempting trap. It's very easy to look upon one's attainments with self-satisfaction and to forget the source of all achievement. Scoring the winning touchdown in a football game, making the highest score on a chemistry test, getting a date with your most attractive class member, owning the latest model of car—all are things that we may think we've earned. In fact, however, the source of all blessings is God. He is where all good things come from.

King Canute never forgot this important lesson—even when his followers were telling him how great he was. From the time of his demonstration at the seashore, he never again wore his crown. Instead, he placed it upon the head of a statue of the crucified Christ. Though he was a powerful king of a whole nation, Canute was willing to give credit where it is due.

➤ Why is it so difficult to give God credit for one's accomplishments?

➤ What accomplishments in your life are you most proud of? Do you give God credit for them?

➤ Think of some physical act that you can perform (as Canute did at the seashore) to demonstrate your dependence on God for your accomplishments. You may do this without any witnesses if you prefer, but think about where all your blessings come from.

DAY 4

"The fruit of righteousness will be peace; the effect of righteousness will be quietness and confidence forever" (Isa. 32:17, NIV).

BARABBAS

In the dying light of the cave,
as the torchlight flickered fitfully,
it was difficult for the three men
to be sure at first that it was he: Barabbas.
They'd always been afraid
a spy could somehow penetrate
their carefully protected brotherhood.

The only recognizable thing
about this man was the angry scar
that slashed its way
from ear to mouth:
that was proof enough
of their old comrade's identity.
Even his voice had changed,
lost its cruel edge.

"I've come back," he said at last,
"to tell you that I'm not coming back.
You're aware, I know,
that I was freed in place
of that Galilean carpenter
who's been creating such a stir.
I thought the jailer was having
one last bit of fun at my expense—
just a sick twist of the knife—
when he came to my cell

and told me I was free to go.
I sat there afraid to move,
thinking it a trick
to torment me in some new way.
    "I'd feel that way even yet,
as if three guards could suddenly appear
at the very mouth of this cave
to drag me back.
But I went to the hill myself,"
he said, his voice almost failing him,
"though I knew the soldiers would be there."
    The day's last slanting rays
suddenly streamed
into the reaches of the cavern,
the setting sun an egg-yolk orange.
    "I went to see this person
who'd taken my place,
look into his face
to see what game he was playing.
I've always said that there are two reasons
for doing the right thing:
the right reason, and the *real* reason.
One look is all it took.
It's no game:
he was dying—and I wasn't."
    He rubbed the scar on his cheek
with the flat of his fist.
Somewhere out in the gathering twilight

a nightingale made its first evening's call.

    "So, here I am,"

he said, looking into each of their faces

as if for the very first time,

"to tell you I won't be coming back.

I'll never be the same again."

    Now he looked past them

toward something beyond.

He smiled.

    "I've created headaches

for the authorities before,

but wait till I begin to share

what I've experienced this day.

I'm sure I'll see a prison cell again—

will probably meet my end

on a cross anyway—

but this time for the *right* reason!"

➤ What does Barabbas say in this poem that suggests that he now has "confidence forever"?

➤ How could Barabbas have this "confidence forever" when it is clear that he knows he will face death?

➤ Write your own short poem in which one of the three men that Barabbas meets in the cave is converted by Barabbas's testimony.

DAY 5

"God so loved the world that he gave his only Son, so that everyone who believes in him will not perish but have eternal life" (John 3:16, NLT).

MY FAVORITE ICON

Looking over the wide variety of commands in my word processing program is always kind of fun. *Who in the world,* I ask myself, *would ever need all this stuff?*

Even with a copy of *Webster's Standard Collegiate* close at hand, I can't always figure out for myself what all these icons mean. The creators of computer hardware and software are ever wrenching the English language in new directions. Thanks to them, we have completely new meanings for old familiar words such as "mouse," "drive," "floppy," and "window."

So I am left to decipher all these features available to me in my word processing program. *I wonder what this one does?* I ask myself. Of course, I wouldn't dream of reading the manual. That's a last resort. Instead, I work by trial and error.

So I browse through the list of commands and play a little game of word association.

"Character mapping," for example. What's that all about? No doubt my character could use a little mapping—a certain amount of guidance maybe—but surely that isn't available in a word processing program, is it?

Here's another one: "manual kerning." OK, "manual" refers to things you can do with your hands. "Kerning?" Didn't I read somewhere that this is the ability to remove your false teeth and cover your nose with your lower lip? Or is that "gurning"? Whatever! If I don't know what it means, I must surely not need it in my word processor.

One of my favorites is "hide family." This one always brings a smile.

I can remember times that I could have really used a button for this. Once when I was a college freshman my grandparents showed up on campus unexpectedly. Thought they'd surprise me with a box of Nana's homemade cookies. When I returned to my dormitory, I found them sitting in the reception room waiting for me.

"Where have you been?" they wanted to know.

"To the library," I answered with a shrug, "researching for a term paper. If I'd known you were coming, I'd have been watching for you. How long have you been waiting?"

"More than an hour," they said. "When we didn't find you here, we got worried and went to the principal's office to ask about you. They didn't even know where you were."

"We don't call him a principal in college, Papa. He's a president!"

"Well, no matter. What kind of school are they running here that they don't know where their students are?"

Unfortunately, the receptionist at the front desk happened to overhear this exchange and felt called upon to share it with half the dorm over the next couple weeks. "Hey, Gary, the principal's office is looking for you!"

That's one time in my life when I could have used a "hide family" button. A "hide self" would have been even better if there were such a thing.

Probably, however, the one word processing command that offers the most positive feelings for me personally is the "undelete" button. This is something that I can understand and embrace with enthusiasm. What a concept!

The word "deleted" sounds so utterly final: gone, misplaced, defunct, lost forever.

But wait. What's this? I can click on this icon, and the three pages that I've just mistakenly deleted come instantly back to the screen. After the heart-stopping realization that I've just deleted a week's work, at a keystroke it just reappears as if by magic. Restored completely. What a lifesaver!

Every time I go through this process, and that's far more often than I care to admit, it suggests a brand-new, twenty-first-century illustration of God's love for humanity. It seems to me the word "undelete" pretty much says it all: "God loved the world so much that He gave His only Son so that whoever believes in Him will be *undeleted* and will live forever" (John 3:16, my own paraphrase).

The parable of the lost sheep could be called the parable of the *deleted* sheep. The good shepherd (maybe we could call him the good computer programmer) has found a way to restore what has been lost. I picture the undelete button as an icon for grace.

The old hymn goes something like this: "There were ninety and nine that safely lay in the shelter of the fold." To read this parable with the assumption that the one lost sheep refers to only drug addicts, bank robbers, and prostitutes is to miss an important opportunity to realize how much God loves you and me. "We all, like sheep, have gone astray" (Isa. 53:6, NIV). We *all* have allowed ourselves—we've chosen—to be deleted! This is what it means to be human.

Yet when God wrote the code for the software program to run our world, He thought of everything ahead of time. He wasn't caught by surprise. There has never been—and never will be—a need for an upgrade. He knew that if He gave humanity freedom of choice, our beautiful world would be infected with a horrendous virus that, if left to itself, would have caused the whole system to crash. Satan is the most malicious hacker imaginable. We're not talking mere mischief here; we're talking outright malevolence. The ultimate in terrorism.

But even before it was needed, God provided an undelete button that gives us a hope that we will not be lost forever. It comes with every program and is available to us all simply for the asking. Now, that's a pretty cool app!

➤ In your own words, explain how God's "undelete button" works to give us hope.

➤ Think over the past week. Is there anything you'd like God to use the undelete button for?

➤ Look for other icons in a word processor program that may have a spiritual application.

Day 6

"A thousand years in your sight are like a day that has just gone by, or like a watch in the night" (Ps. 90:4, NIV).

HOURGLASS

This hourglass—
    misnamed—
is nothing more than someone else's measure
    of a soft, three-minute egg.
Yet the solitary moments
    jostle grain upon grain
        like single platelets
        through the thinnest capillary—
    and form a perfect cone of time.
I'd like to give its neck
    a satisfying snap
    and let the particles of time
        sift into my open palm.
I'd feel the heft
    and texture of it,
then throw it to the wind—
    would do it, too,
        if it belonged to me—
        if it were indeed *ourglass*
        to do with as we wish.

➤ How do Psalm 90:4 and "Hourglass" agree or disagree on the role of time in the human experience?

➤ Explain in your own words what is meant by the line "if it were indeed ourglass."

➤ Imagine you could time travel. What event in the Bible would you like to experience personally? Why?

DAY 7

"O Lord, what is man that you care for him, the son of man that you think of him?" (Ps. 144:3, NIV).

MAKING IT PERSONAL

Try one or more of the following activities as you complete this week's consideration of the subject of being human:

- Go to a public place where there is a lot of human activity (mall, train station, intersection, etc.). Then close your eyes and listen to the sounds going on around you. Think about what these sounds suggest about what people are like.

- Select an object lesson from nature to illustrate an aspect of being human. Using this as a focus, write a short psalm of your own.

- In some art form (drawing, painting, sculpture, collage, etc.), produce your own portrayal of what it means to be human.

- In several versions, read prayerfully the biblical account of the creation of humanity (Gen. 1:26, 27). Compose a piece of music that communicates this event, and offer to perform it for a church meeting.

- Select two or three scriptural references that you think express the dependence of humanity on God, and use them as signatures to appear on each e-mail you send.

Other books by Gary B. Swanson:

The Moose, the Goose, and the Kingdom of God
My Father Owns This Place
Surprise Me!
The Great Tennis Shoe Dilemma

To order, call 1-800-765-6955.

Visit us at www.reviewandherald.com for information on other
Review and Herald® products.